THE STORY OF
THE TREASURE SEEKERS

Also in Armada by E. Nesbit

THE RAILWAY CHILDREN

Other Famous Stories in Armada

THE STORY OF
THE TREASURE SEEKERS

*Being the Adventures of the Bastable Children
in Search of a Fortune*

By

E. NESBIT

With Illustrations by
GORDON BROWNE

Armada

The Story of the Treasure Seekers was first
published in 1899.
This edition was first published in hardback
in 1958 by Ernest Benn Ltd.
First published in Armada in 1982 by
Fontana Paperbacks, 14 St James's Place,
London SW1A 1PS.

Printed in Great Britain by
The Anchor Press Ltd, Tiptree,
Colchester, Essex.

CONTENTS

I don't suppose he was used to politeness from boys

LIST OF ILLUSTRATIONS

CHAPTER I

THE COUNCIL OF WAYS AND MEANS

THIS IS the story of the different ways we looked for treasure, and I think when you have read it you will see that we were not lazy about the looking.

There are some things I must tell before I begin to tell about the treasure-seeking, because I have read books myself, and I know how beastly it is when a story begins, " 'Alas!' said Hildegarde with a deep sigh, 'we must look our last on this ancestral home' "—and then someone else says something—and you don't know for pages and pages where the home is, or who Hildegarde is, or anything about it. Our ancestral home is in the Lewisham Road. It is semi-detached and has a garden, not a large one. We are the Bastables. There are six of us besides Father. Our Mother is dead, and if you think we don't care because I don't tell you much about her you only show that you do not understand people at all. Dora is the eldest. Then Oswald—and then Dicky. Oswald won the Latin prize at his preparatory school—and Dicky is good at sums. Alice and Noël are twins. They are ten, and Horace Octavius is my youngest brother. It is one of us that tells this story—but I shall not tell you which: only at the very end perhaps I will. While the story is going on you may be trying to guess, only I bet you don't.

It was Oswald who first thought of looking for treasure. Oswald often thinks of very interesting things. And directly he thought of it he did not keep it to himself, as some boys would have done, but he told the others, and said—

"I'll tell you what, we must go and seek for treasure: it

is always what you do to restore the fallen fortunes of your House."

Dora said it was all very well. She often says that. She was trying to mend a large hole in one of Noël's stockings. He tore it on a nail when we were playing shipwrecked mariners on top of the chicken-house the day H. O. fell off and cut his chin: he has the scar still. Dora is the only one of us who ever tries to mend anything. Alice tries to make things sometimes. Once she knitted a red scarf for Noël because his chest is delicate, but it was much wider at one end than the other, and he wouldn't wear it. So we used it as a pennon, and it did very well, because most of our things are black or grey since Mother died; and scarlet was a nice change. Father does not like you to ask for new things. That was one way we had of knowing that the fortunes of the ancient House of Bastable were really fallen. Another way was that there was no more pocket-money— except a penny now and then to the little ones, and people did not come to dinner any more, like they used to, with pretty dresses, driving up in cabs—and the carpets got holes in them—and when the legs came off things they were not sent to be mended, and we gave up having the gardener except for the front garden, and not that very often. And the silver in the big oak plate-chest that is lined with green baize all went away to the shop to have the dents and scratches taken out of it, and it never came back. We think Father hadn't enough money to pay the silver man for taking out the dents and scratches. The new spoons and forks were yellowy-white, and not so heavy as the old ones, and they never shone after the first day or two.

Father was very ill after Mother died; and while he was ill his business-partner went to Spain—and there was never much money afterwards. I don't know why. Then the servants left and there was only one, a General. A great deal of your comfort and happiness depends on having a good General. The last but one was nice: she used to make jolly good currant puddings for us, and let us have the dish on the floor and pretend it was a wild boar we were killing with our forks. But the General we have now nearly always makes sago puddings, and they are the watery kind, and you cannot pretend anything with them, not even islands, like you do with porridge.

Then we left off going to school, and Father said we should go to a good school as soon as he could manage it. He said a holiday would do us all good. We thought he was right, but we wished he had told us he couldn't afford it. For of course we knew.

Then a great many people used to come to the door with envelopes with no stamps on them, and sometimes they got very angry, and said they were calling for the last time before putting it in other hands. I asked Eliza what that meant, and she kindly explained it to me, and I was so sorry for Father.

And once a long, blue paper came; a policeman brought it, and we were so frightened. But Father said it was all right, only when he went up to kiss the girls after they were in bed they said he had been crying, though I'm sure that's not true. Because only cowards and snivellers cry, and my Father is the bravest man in the world.

So you see it was time we looked for treasure; and Oswald said so, and Dora said it was all very well. But the others agreed with Oswald. So we held a council. Dora was in the chair—the big dining-room chair, that we let the fireworks off from, the Fifth of November when he had the measles and couldn't do it in the garden. The hole has never been mended, so now we have that chair in the nursery, and I think it was cheap at the blowing-up we boys got when the hole was burnt.

"We must do something," said Alice, "because the exchequer is empty." She rattled the money-box as she spoke, and it really did rattle because we always keep the bad sixpence in it for luck.

"Yes—but what shall we do?" said Dicky. "It's so jolly easy to say let's do *something*." Dicky always wants everything settled exactly. Father calls him the Definite Article.

"Let's read all the books again. We shall get lots of ideas out of them." It was Noël who suggested this, but we made him shut up, because we knew well enough he only wanted to get back to his old books. Noël is a poet. He sold some of his poetry once—and it was printed, but that does not come in this part of the story.

Then Dicky said, "Look here. We'll be quite quiet for ten minutes by the clock—and each think of some way to find treasure. And when we've thought we'll try all the ways one after the other, beginning with the eldest."

"I shan't be able to think in ten minutes, make it half an hour," said H. O. His real name is Horace Octavius, but we call him H. O. because of the advertisement, and it's not so very long ago he was afraid to pass the hoarding where it says "Eat H. O." in big letters. He says it was when he was a little boy, but I remember last Christmas but one, he woke in the middle of the night crying and howling, and they said it was the pudding. But he told me afterwards he had been dreaming that they really *had* come to eat H. O., and it couldn't have been the pudding, when you come to think of it, because it was so very plain.

Well, we made it half an hour—and we all sat quiet, and thought and thought And I made up my mind before two minutes were over, and I saw the others had, all but Dora, who is always an awful time over everything. I got pins and needles in my leg from sitting still so long, and when it was seven minutes H. O. cried out—

"Oh, it must be more than half an hour!"

H.O. is eight years old, but he cannot tell the clock yet. Oswald could tell the clock when he was six.

We all stretched ourselves and began to speak at once, but Dora put up her hands to her ears and said—

"One at a time, please. We aren't playing Babel." (It is a very good game. Did you ever play it?)

So Dora made us all sit in a row on the floor, in ages, and then she pointed at us with the finger that had the brass thimble on. Her silver one got lost when the last General but two went away. We think she must have forgotten it was Dora's and put it in her box by mistake. She was a very forgetful girl. She used to forget what she had spent money on, so that the change was never quite right.

Oswald spoke first. "I think we might stop people on Blackheath—with crape masks and horse-pistols—and say 'Your money or your life! Resistance is useless, we are armed to the teeth'—like Dick Turpin and Claude Duval. It wouldn't matter about not having horses, because coaches have gone out too."

Dora screwed up her nose the way she always does when she is going to talk like the good elder sister in books, and said, "That would be very wrong: it's like pickpocketing or taking pennies out of Father's greatcoat when it's hanging in the hall."

I must say I don't think she need have said that, especially before the little ones—for it was when I was only four.

But Oswald was not going to let her see he cared, so he said—

"Oh, very well. I can think of lots of other ways. We could rescue an old gentleman from deadly Highwaymen."

"There aren't any," said Dora.

"Oh, well, it's all the same—from deadly peril, then. There's plenty of that. Then he would turn out to be the

Prince of Wales, and he would say, 'My noble, my cherished preserver! Here is a million pounds a year. Rise up, Sir Oswald Bastable'."

But the others did not seem to think so, and it was Alice's turn to say.

She said, "I think we might try the divining-rod. I'm sure I could do it. I've often read about it. You hold a stick in your hands, and when you come to where there is gold underneath the stick kicks about. So you know. And you dig."

"Oh," said Dora suddenly, "I have an idea. But I'll say last. I hope the divining-rod isn't wrong. I believe it's wrong in the Bible."

"So is eating pork and ducks," said Dicky. "You can't go by that."

"Anyhow, we'll try the other ways first," said Dora. "Now, H. O."

"Let's be Bandits," said H. O. "I dare say it's wrong, but it would be fun pretending."

"I'm sure it's wrong," said Dora.

And Dicky said she thought everything wrong. She said she didn't, and Dicky was very disagreeable. So Oswald had to make peace, and he said—

"Dora needn't play if she doesn't want to. Nobody asked her. And, Dicky, don't be an idiot: do dry up and let's hear what Noël's idea is.

Dora and Dicky did not look pleased, but I kicked Noël under the table to make him hurry up, and then he said he didn't think he wanted to play any more. That's the worst of it. The others are so jolly ready to quarrel. I told Noël to be a man and not a snivelling pig, and at last he said he had not made up his mind whether he would print his poetry in a book and sell it, or find a princess and marry her.

"Whichever it is," he added, "none of you shall want for

anything, though Oswald did kick me, and say I was a snivelling pig."

"I didn't," said Oswald, "I told you not to be." And Alice explained to him that that was quite the opposite of what he thought. So he agreed to drop it.

Then Dicky spoke.

"You must all of you have noticed the advertisements in the papers, telling you that ladies and gentlemen can easily earn two pounds a week in their spare time, and to send two shillings for sample and instructions, carefully packed free from observation. Now that we don't go to school all our time is spare time. So I should think we could easily earn twenty pounds a week each. That would do us very well. We'll try some of the other things first, and directly we have any money we'll send for the sample and instructions. And I have another idea, but I must think about it before I say."

We all said, "Out with it—what's the other idea?"

But Dicky said, "No." That is Dicky all over. He never will show you anything he's making till it's quite finished, and the same with his innermost thoughts. But he is pleased if you seem to want to know, so Oswald said—

"Keep your silly old secret, then. Now, Dora, drive ahead. We've all said except you."

Then Dora jumped up and dropped the stocking and the thimble (it rolled away, and we did not find it for days), and said—

"Let's try my way *now*. Besides, I'm the eldest, so it's only fair. Let's dig for treasure. Not any tiresome divining-rod—but just plain digging. People who dig for treasure always find it. And then we shall be rich and we needn't try your ways at all. Some of them are rather difficult: and I'm certain some of them are wrong—and we must always remember that wrong things——"

But we told her to shut up and come on, and she did.

I couldn't help wondering as we went down to the garden, why Father had never thought of digging there for treasure instead of going to his beastly office every day.

CHAPTER II

DIGGING FOR TREASURE

I AM AFRAID the last chapter was rather dull. It is always dull in books when people talk and talk, and don't do anything, but I was obliged to put it in, or else you wouldn't have understood all the rest. The best part of books is when things are happening. That is the best part of real things too. This is why I shall not tell you in this story about all the days when nothing happened. You will not catch me saying, "thus the sad days passed slowly by"—or "the years rolled on their weary course"—or "time went on"—because it is silly; of course times goes on—whether you say so or not. So I shall just tell you the nice, interesting parts—and in between you will understand that we had our meals and got up and went to bed, and dull things like that. It would be sickening to write all that down, though of course it happens. I said so to Albert-next-door's uncle, who writes books, and he said, "Quite right, that's what we call selection, a necessity of true art." And he is very clever indeed. So you see.

I have often thought that if the people who write books for children knew a little more it would be better. I shall not tell you anything about us except what I should like to know about if I was reading the story and you were writing it. Albert's uncle says I ought to have put this in the preface, but I never read prefaces, and it is not much good writing things just for people to skip. I wonder other authors have never thought of this.

Well, when we had agreed to dig for treasure we all went down into the cellar and lighted the gas. Oswald would have liked to dig there, but it is stone flags. We looked among the old boxes and broken chairs and fenders and empty bottles and things, and at last we found the spades we had to dig in the sand with when we went to the seaside three years ago. They are not silly, babyish, wooden spades, that split if you look at them, but good iron, with a blue mark across the top of the iron part, and yellow wooden handles. We wasted a little time getting them dusted, because the girls wouldn't dig with spades that had cobwebs on them. Girls would never do for African explorers or anything like that, they are too beastly particular.

It was no use doing the thing by halves. We marked out a sort of square in the mouldy part of the garden, about three yards across, and began to dig. But we found nothing except worms and stones—and the ground was very hard.

So we thought we'd try another part of the garden, and we found a place in the big round flower bed, where the ground was much softer. We thought we'd make a smaller hole to begin with, and it was much better. We dug and dug and dug, and it was jolly hard work! We got very hot digging, but we found nothing.

Presently Albert-next-door looked over the wall. We do not like him very much, but we let him play with us sometimes, because his father is dead, and you must not be unkind to orphans, even if their mothers are alive. Albert is always very tidy. He wears frilly collars and velvet knickerbockers. I can't think how he can bear to.

So we said, "Hullo!"

And he said, "What are you up to?"

"We're digging for treasure," said Alice; "an ancient parchment revealed to us the place of concealment. Come over and help us. When we have dug deep enough we shall find a great pot of red clay, full of gold and precious jewels."

Albert-next-door only sniggered and said, "What silly nonsense!" He cannot play properly at all. It is very strange, because he has a very nice uncle. You see, Albert-next-door doesn't care for reading, and he has not read nearly so many books as we have, so he is very foolish and ignorant, but it cannot be helped, and you just have to put up with it when you want him to do anything. Besides, it is wrong to be angry with people for not being so clever as you are yourself. It is not always their faults.

So Oswald said, "Come and dig! Then you shall share the treasure when we've found it."

But he said, "I shan't—I don't like digging—and I'm just going in to my tea."

"Come along and dig, there's a good boy," Alice said. "You can use my spade. It's much the best——"

So he came along and dug, and when once he was over the wall we kept him at it, and we worked as well, of course, and the hole got deep. Pincher worked too—he is our dog and he is very good at digging. He digs for rats in the dust-bin sometimes, and gets very dirty. But we love our dog, even when his face wants washing.

"I expect we shall have to make a tunnel," Oswald said, "to reach the rich treasure." So he jumped into the hole and began to dig at one side. After that we took it in turns to dig at the tunnel, and Pincher was most useful in scraping the earth out of the tunnel—he does it with his back feet when you say "Rats!" and he digs with his front ones, and burrows with his nose as well.

At last the tunnel was nearly a yard long, and big enough to creep along to find the treasure, if only it had been a bit longer. Now it was Albert's turn to go in and dig, but he funked it.

"Take your turn like a man," said Oswald—nobody can say that Oswald doesn't take his turn like a man. But Albert wouldn't. So we had to make him, because it was only fair.

"It's quite easy," Alice said. "You just crawl in and dig

with your hands. Then when you come out we can scrape out what you've done, with the spades. Come—be a man. You won't notice it being dark in the tunnel if you shut your eyes tight. We've all been in except Dora—and she doesn't like worms."

"I don't like worms neither." Albert-next-door said this; but we remembered how he had picked a fat red and black worm up in his fingers and thrown it at Dora only the day before.

So we put him in.

But he would not go in head first, the proper way, and dig with his hands as we had done, and though Oswald was angry at the time, for he hates snivellers, yet afterwards he owned that perhaps it was just as well. You should never be afraid to own that perhaps you were mistaken—but it is cowardly to do it unless you are quite sure you are in the wrong.

"Let me go in feet first," said Albert-next-door. "I'll dig with my boots—I will truly, honour bright."

So we let him get in feet first—and he did it very slowly and at last he was in, and only his head sticking out into the hole; and all the rest of him in the tunnel.

"Now dig with your boots," said Oswald; "and, Alice, do catch hold of Pincher, he'll be digging again in another minute, and perhaps it would be uncomfortable for Albert if Pincher threw the mould into his eyes."

You should always try to think of these little things. Thinking of other people's comfort makes them like you. Alice held Pincher, and we all shouted, "Kick! dig with your feet, for all you're worth!"

So Albert-next-door began to dig with his feet, and we stood on the ground over him, waiting, and all in a minute the ground gave way, and we tumbled together in a heap: and when we got up there was a little shallow hollow where

we had been standing, and Albert-next-door was underneath, stuck quite fast, because the roof of the tunnel had
tumbled in on him. He is a horribly unlucky boy to have
anything to do with.

It was dreadful the way he cried and screamed, though
he had to own it didn't hurt, only it was rather heavy and he
couldn't move his legs. We would have dug him out all right
enough, in time, but he screamed so we were afraid the
police would come, so Dicky climbed over the wall, to tell
the cook there to tell Albert-next-door's uncle he had been
buried by mistake, and to come and help dig him out.

Dicky was a long time gone. We wondered what had become of him, and all the while the screaming went on and
on, for we had taken the loose earth off Albert's face so that
he could scream quite easily and comfortably.

Presently Dicky came back and Albert-next-door's uncle
came with him. He has very long legs, and his hair is light
and his face is brown. He has been to sea, but now he writes
books. I like him.

He told his nephew to stow it, so Albert did, and then he
asked him if he was hurt—and Albert had to say he wasn't,
for though he is a coward, and very unlucky, he is not a liar
like some boys are.

"This promises to be a protracted if agreeable task," said
Albert-next-door's uncle, rubbing his hands and looking at
the hole with Albert's head in it. "I will get another spade,"
so he fetched the big spade out of the next-door garden tool-
shed, and began to dig his nephew out.

"Mind you keep very still," he said, "or I might chunk
a bit out of you with the spade." Then after a while he
said—

"I confess that I am not absolutely insensible to the drama-
tic interest of the situation. My curiosity is excited. I own
that I should like to know how my nephew happened to be

buried. But don't tell me if you'd rather not. I suppose no force was used?"

"Only moral force," said Alice. They used to talk a lot about moral force at the High School where she went, and in case you don't know what it means I'll tell you that it is making people do what they don't want to, just by slanging them, or laughing at them, or promising them things if they're good.

"Only moral force, eh?" said Albert-next-door's uncle. "Well?"

"Well," Dora said, "I'm very sorry it happened to Albert —I'd rather it had been one of us. It would have been my turn to go into the tunnel, only I don't like worms, so they let me off. You see we were digging for treasure."

"Yes," said Alice, "and I think we were just coming to the underground passage that leads to the secret hoard, when the tunnel fell in on Albert. He *is* so unlucky," and she sighed.

Then Albert-next-door began to scream again, and his uncle wiped his face—his own face, not Albert's—with his silk handkerchief, and then he put it in his trousers pocket. It seems a strange place to put a handkerchief, but he had his coat and waistcoat off and I suppose he wanted the handkerchief handy. Digging is warm work.

He told Albert-next-door to drop it, or he wouldn't proceed further in the matter, so Albert stopped screaming, and presently his uncle finished digging him out. Albert did look so funny, with his hair all dusty and his velvet suit covered with mould and his face muddy with earth and crying.

We all said how sorry we were, but he wouldn't say a word back to us. He was most awfully sick to think he'd been the one buried, when it might just as well have been one of us. I felt myself that it was hard lines.

"So you were digging for treasure," said Albert-next-door's uncle, wiping his face again with his handkerchief. "Well, I fear that your chances of success are small. I have made a careful study of the whole subject. What I don't know about buried treasure is not worth knowing. And I never knew more than one coin buried in any one garden —and that is generally—— Hullo—what's that?"

He pointed to something shining in the hole he had just dragged Albert out of. Oswald picked it up. It was a half-crown. We looked at each other, speechless with surprise and delight, like in books.

"Well, that's lucky, at all events," said Albert-next-door's uncle. "Let's see, that's fivepence each for you."

"It's fourpence—something; I can't do fractions," said Dicky; "there are seven of us, you see."

"Oh, you count Albert as one of yourselves on this occasion, eh?"

"Of course," said Alice; "and I say, he was buried after all. Why shouldn't we let him have the odd somethings, and we'll have fourpence each."

We all agreed to this, and told Albert-next-door we would bring his share as soon as we could get the half-crown changed. He cheered up a little at that, and his uncle wiped his face again—he did look hot—and began to put on his coat and waistcoat.

When he had done it he stooped and picked up something. He held it up, and you will hardly believe it, but it is quite true—it was another half-crown!

"To think that there should be two!" he said; "in all my experience of buried treasure I never heard of such a thing!"

I wish Albert-next-door's uncle would come treasure-seeking with us regularly; he must have very sharp eyes: for Dora says she was looking just the minute before at the very place where the second half-crown was picked up from, and *she* never saw it.

CHAPTER III

BEING DETECTIVES

THE NEXT thing that happened to us was very interesting. It was as real as the half-crowns—not just pretending. I shall try to write it as like a real book as I can. Of course we have read Mr. Sherlock Holmes, as well as the yellow-covered books with pictures outside that are so badly printed; and you get them for fourpence-halfpenny at the bookstall when the corners of them are beginning to curl up and get dirty, with people looking to see how the story ends when they are waiting for trains. I think this is most unfair to the boy at the bookstall. The books are written by a gentleman named Gaboriau, and Albert's uncle says they are the worst translations in the world—and written in vile English. Of course they're not like Kipling, but they're jolly good stories. And we had just been reading a book by Dick Diddlington—that's not his right name, but I know all about libel actions, so I shall not say what his name is really, because his books are rot. Only they put it into our heads to do what I am going to narrate.

It was in September, and we were not to go to the seaside because it is so expensive, even if you go to Sheerness, where it is all tin cans and old boots and no sand at all. But every one else went, even the people next door—not Albert's side, but the other. Their servant told Eliza they were all going to Scarborough, and next day sure enough all the blinds were down and the shutters up, and the milk was not left any more. There is a big horse-chestnut tree between their garden and ours, very useful for getting conkers out of and for making stuff to rub on your chilblains. This prevented our seeing whether the blinds were down at the back as well, but Dicky climbed to the top of the tree and looked, and they were.

It was jolly hot weather, and very stuffy indoors—we used to play a good deal in the garden. We made a tent out of the kitchen clothes-horse and some blankets off our beds, and though it was quite as hot in the tent as in the house it was a very different sort of hotness. Albert's uncle called it the Turkish Bath. It is not nice to be kept from the seaside, but we know that we have much to be thankful for. We might be poor little children living in a crowded alley where even at summer noon hardly a ray of sunlight penetrates; clothed in rags and with bare feet—though I do not mind holes in my clothes myself, and bare feet would not be at all bad in this sort of weather. Indeed we do, sometimes, when we are playing at things which require it. It was ship-wrecked mariners that day, I remember, and we were all in the blanket tent. We had just finished eating the things we had saved, at the peril of our lives, from the fast-sinking vessel. They were rather nice things. Twopennyworth of coconut candy—it was got in Greenwich, where it is four ounces a penny—three apples, some macaroni—the straight sort that is so useful to suck things through—some raw rice, and a large piece of cold suet pudding that Alice nicked from the larder when she went to get the rice and macaroni. And when we had finished some one said—

"I should like to be a detective."

I wish to be quite fair, but I cannot remember exactly who said it. Oswald thinks he said it, and Dora says it was Dicky, but Oswald is too much of a man to quarrel about a little thing like that.

"I should like to be a detective," said—perhaps it was Dicky, but I think not—"and find out strange and hidden crimes."

"You have to be much cleverer than you are," said H.O.

"Not so very," Alice said, "because when you've read the books you know what the things mean: the red hair on the handle of the knife, or the grains of white powder on the velvet collar of the villain's overcoat. I believe we could do it."

"I shouldn't like to have anything to do with murders," said Dora; "somehow it doesn't seem safe——"

"And it always ends in the poor murderer being hanged," said Alice.

We explained to her why murderers have to be hanged, but she only said, "I don't care. I'm sure no one would ever do murdering *twice*. Think of the blood and things, and what you would see when you woke up in the night! I shouldn't mind being a detective to lie in wait for a gang of coiners, now, and spring upon them unawares, and secure them—single-handed, you know, or with only my faithful bloodhound."

She stroked Pincher's ears, but he had gone to sleep because he knew well enough that all the suet pudding was finished. He is a very sensible dog.

"You always get hold of the wrong end of the stick," Oswald said. "You can't choose what crimes you'll be a detective about. You just have to get a suspicious circumstance, and then you look for a clue and follow it up. Whether it turns out a murder or a missing will is just a fluke."

"That's one way," Dicky said. "Another is to get a paper and find two advertisements or bits of news that fit. Like this: 'Young Lady Missing,' and then it tells about all the clothes she had on, and the gold locket she wore, and the colour of her hair, and all that; and then in another piece of the paper you see, 'Gold locket found,' and then it all comes out."

We sent H. O. for the paper at once, but we could not

make any of the things fit in. The two best were about how some burglars broke into a place in Holloway where they made preserved tongues and invalid delicacies, and carried off a lot of them. And on another page there was "Mysterious deaths in Holloway."

Oswald thought there was something in it, and so did Albert's uncle when we asked him, but the others thought not, so Oswald agreed to drop it. Besides, Holloway is a long way off. All the time we were talking about the paper Alice seemed to be thinking about something else, and when we had done she said—

"I believe we might be detectives ourselves, but I should not like to get anybody into trouble."

"Not murderers or robbers?" Dicky asked.

"It wouldn't be murderers," she said; "but I *have* noticed something strange. Only I feel a little frightened. Let's ask Albert's uncle first."

Alice is a jolly sight too fond of asking grown-up people things. And we all said it was tommy-rot, and she was to tell us.

"Well, promise you won't do anything without me," Alice said, and we promised. Then she said—

"This is a dark secret, and any one who thinks it is better not to be involved in a career of crime-discovery had better go away ere yet it be too late."

So Dora said she had had enough of tents, and she was going to look at the shops. H. O. went with her because he had twopence to spend. They thought it was only a game of Alice's, but Oswald knew by the way she spoke. He can nearly always tell. And when people are not telling the truth Oswald generally knows by the way they look with their eyes. Oswald is not proud of being able to do this. He knows it is through no merit of his own that he is much cleverer than some people.

When they had gone, the rest of us got closer together and said—

"Now then."

"Well," Alice said, "you know the house next door? The people have gone to Scarborough. And the house is shut up. But last night *I saw a light in the windows.*"

We asked her how and when, because her room is in the front, and she couldn't possibly have seen. And then she said—

"I'll tell you if you boys will promise not ever to go fishing again without me."

So we had to promise.

Then she said—

"It was last night. I had forgotten to feed my rabbits, and I woke up and remembered it. And I was afraid I should find them dead in the morning, like Oswald did."

"It wasn't my fault," Oswald said; "there was something the matter with the beasts. I fed them right enough."

Alice said she didn't mean that, and she went on—

"I came down into the garden, and I saw a light in the house, and dark figures moving about. I thought perhaps it was burglars, but Father hadn't come home, and Eliza had gone to bed, so I couldn't do anything. Only I thought perhaps I would tell the rest of you."

"Why didn't you tell us this morning?" Noël asked. And Alice explained that she did not want to get any one into trouble, even burglars. "But we might watch to-night," she said, "and see if we see the light again."

"They might have been burglars," Noël said. He was sucking the last bit of his macaroni. "You know the people next door are very grand. They won't know us—and they go out in a real private carriage sometimes. And they have an 'At Home' day, and people come in cabs. I daresay they have piles of plate and jewellery and rich brocades, and furs of price and things like that. Let us keep watch to-night."

"It's no use watching to-night," Dicky said; "if it's only burglars they won't come again. But there are other things besides burglars that are discovered in empty houses where lights are seen moving."

"You mean coiners," said Oswald at once. "I wonder what the reward is for setting the police on their track?"

Dicky thought it ought to be something fat, because coiners are always a desperate gang; and the machinery they make the coins with is so heavy and handy for knocking down detectives.

Then it was tea-time, and we went in; and Dora and H. O. had clubbed their money together and bought a melon; quite a big one, and only a little bit squashy at one end. It was very good, and then we washed the seeds and made things with them and with pins and cotton. And nobody said any more about watching the house next door.

Only when we went to bed Dicky took off his coat and waistcoat, but he stopped at his braces and said—

"What about the coiners?"

Oswald had taken off his collar and tie, and he was just going to say the same, so he said, "Of course I meant to watch, only my collar's rather tight, so I thought I'd take it off first."

Dicky said he did not think the girls ought to be in it, because there might be danger, but Oswald reminded him that they had promised Alice, and that a promise is a sacred thing, even when you'd much rather not. So Oswald got Alice alone under pretence of showing her a caterpillar— Dora does not like them, and she screamed and ran away when Oswald offered to show it her. Then Oswald explained, and Alice agreed to come and watch if she could. This made us later than we ought to have been, because

Alice had to wait till Dora was quiet and then creep out very slowly, for fear of the boards creaking. The girls sleep with their room-door open for fear of burglars. Alice had kept on her clothes under her nightgown when Dora wasn't looking, and presently they got down, creeping past Father's study, and out at the glass door that leads on to the veranda and the iron steps into the garden. And we went down very quietly, and got into the chestnut-tree, and then I felt that we had only been playing what Albert's uncle calls our favourite instrument—I mean the Fool. For the house next door was as dark as dark. Then suddenly we heard a sound —it came from the gate at the end of the garden. All the gardens have gates; they lead into a kind of lane that runs behind them. It is a sort of back way, very convenient when you don't want to say exactly where you are going. We heard the gate at the end of the next garden click, and Dicky nudged Alice so that she would have fallen out of the tree if it had not been for Oswald's extraordinary presence of mind. Oswald squeezed Alice's arm tight, and we all looked; and the others were rather frightened because really we had not exactly expected anything to happen except perhaps a light. But now a muffled figure, shrouded in a dark cloak, came swiftly up the path of the next-door garden. And we could see that under its cloak the figure carried a mysterious burden. The figure was dressed to look like a woman in a sailor hat.

We held our breath as it passed under the tree where we were, and then it tapped very gently on the back door and was let in, and then a light appeared in the window of the downstairs back breakfast-room. But the shutters were up.

Dicky said, "My eye!" and wouldn't the others be sick to think they hadn't been in this! But Alice didn't half like it—and as she is a girl I do not blame her. Indeed, I thought myself at first that perhaps it would be better to retire for the present, and return later with a strongly armed force.

"It's not burglars," Alice whispered; "the mysterious stranger was bringing things in, not taking them out. They must be coiners—and oh, Oswald!—don't let's! The things they coin with must hurt very much. Do let's go to bed!"

But Dicky said he was going to see; if there was a reward for finding out things like this he would like to have the reward.

"They locked the back door," he whispered, "I heard it go. And I could look in quite well through the holes in the shutters and be back over the wall long before they'd got the door open, even if they started to do it at once."

There were holes at the top of the shutters the shape of hearts, and the yellow light came out through them as well as through the chinks of the shutters.

Oswald said if Dicky went he should, because he was the eldest; and Alice said, "If any one goes it ought to be me, because I thought of it."

So Oswald said, "Well, go then"; and she said, "Not for anything!" And she begged us not to, and we talked about it in the tree till we were all quite hoarse with whispering.

At last we decided on a plan of action.

Alice was to stay in the tree, and scream "Murder!" if anything happened. Dicky and I were to get down into the next garden and take it in turns to peep.

So we got down as quietly as we could, but the tree made much more noise than it does in the day, and several times we paused, fearing that all was discovered. But nothing happened.

There was a pile of red flower-pots under the window and one very large one was on the window-ledge. It seemed as if it was the hand of Destiny had placed it there, and the geranium in it was dead, and there was nothing to stop your standing on it—so Oswald did. He went first because he is the eldest, and though Dicky tried to stop him because he thought of it first it could not be, on account of not being able to say anything.

So Oswald stood on the flower-pot and tried to look through one of the holes. He did not really expect to see the coiners at their fell work, though he had pretended to when we were talking in the tree. But if he had seen them pouring the base molten metal into tin moulds the shape of half-crowns he would not have been half so astonished as he was at the spectacle now revealed.

At first he could see little, because the hole had unfortunately been made a little too high, so that the eye of the detective could only see the Prodigal Son in a shiny frame on the opposite wall. But Oswald held on to the window-frame and stood on tiptoe and then he *saw*.

There was no furnace, and no base metal, no bearded men in leathern aprons with tongs and things, but just a table with a table-cloth on it for supper, and a tin of salmon and a lettuce and some bottled beer. And there on a chair was the cloak and the hat of the mysterious stranger, and the two people sitting at the table were the two youngest grown-up daughters of the lady next door, and one of them was saying—

"So I got the salmon three-halfpence cheaper, and the lettuces are only six a penny in the Broadway, just fancy! We must save as much as ever we can on our housekeeping money if we want to go away decent next year."

And the other said, "I wish we could *all* go *every* year, or else—— Really, I almost wish——"

And all the time Oswald was looking Dicky was pulling at his jacket to make him get down and let Dicky have a squint. And just as she said "I almost," Dicky pulled too hard and Oswald felt himself toppling on the giddy verge of the big flower-pot. Putting forth all his strength our hero strove to recover his equi- what's-its-name, but it was now lost beyond recall.

"You've done it this time!" he said, then he fell heavily among the flower-pots piled below. He heard them crash and rattle and crack, and then his head struck against an iron pillar used for holding up the next-door veranda. His eyes closed and he knew no more.

Now you will perhaps expect that at this moment Alice would have cried "Murder!" If you think so you little know what girls are. Directly she was left alone in that tree she made a bolt to tell Albert's uncle all about it and bring him to our rescue in case the coiners' gang was a very desperate one. And just when I fell, Albert's uncle was getting over the wall. Alice never screamed at all when Oswald fell, but Dicky thinks he heard Albert's uncle say, "Confound those kids!" which would not have been kind or polite, so I hope he did not say it.

The people next door did not come out to see what the row was. Albert's uncle did not wait for them to come out. He picked up Oswald and carried the insensible body of the gallant young detective to the wall, laid it on the top, and then climbed over and bore his lifeless burden into our house and put it on the sofa in Father's study. Father was out, so we needn't have *crept* so when we were getting into the garden. Then Oswald was restored to consciousness, and his head tied up, and sent to bed, and next day there was a lump on his young brow as big as a turkey's egg, and very uncomfortable.

Albert's uncle came in next day and talked to each of us separately. To Oswald he said many unpleasant things about ungentlemanly to spy on ladies, and about minding your own business; and when I began to tell him what I had heard he told me to shut up, and altogether he made me more uncomfortable than the bump did.

Oswald did not say anything to any one, but next day, as the shadows of eve were falling, he crept away, and wrote on a piece of paper. "I want to speak to you," and shoved it through the hole like a heart in the top of the next-door shutters.

And the youngest young lady put an eye to the heart-shaped hole, and then opened the shutter and said "Well?" very crossly.

Then Oswald said—

"I am very sorry, and I beg your pardon. We wanted to be detectives, and we thought a gang of coiners infested your house, so we looked through your window last night. I saw the lettuce, and I heard what you said about the salmon being three-halfpence cheaper, and I know it is very dishonourable to pry into other people's secrets, especially ladies', and I never will again if you will forgive me this once."

Then the lady frowned and then she laughed, and then she said—

"So it was *you* tumbling into the flower-pots last night? We thought it was burglars. It frightened us horribly. Why, what a bump on your poor head!"

And then she talked to me a bit, and presently she said she and her sister had not wished people to know they were at home, because—— And then she stopped short and grew very red, and I said, "I thought you were all at Scarborough; your servant told Eliza so. Why didn't you want people to know you were at home?"

The lady got redder still, and then she laughed and said—

"Never mind the reason why. I hope your head doesn't hurt much. Thank you for your nice, manly little speech. *You've* nothing to be ashamed of, at any rate." Then she kissed me, and I did not mind. And then she said, "Run away now, dear. I'm going to—I'm going to pull up the blinds and open the shutters, and I want to do it at *once*, before it gets dark, so that every one can see we're at home, and not at Scarborough."

CHAPTER IV

GOOD HUNTING

WHEN WE had got that five shillings by digging for treasure we ought, by rights, to have tried Dicky's idea of answering the advertisement about ladies and gentlemen and spare time and two pounds a week, but there were several things we rather wanted.

Dora wanted a new pair of scissors, and she said she was going to get them with her eightpence. But Alice said—

"You ought to get her those, Oswald because you know you broke the points off hers getting the marble out of the brass thimble."

It was quite true, though I had almost forgotten it, but then it was H. O. who jammed the marble into the thimble first of all. So I said—

"It's H. O.'s fault as much as mine, anyhow. Why shouldn't he pay?"

Oswald didn't so much mind paying for the beastly scissors, but he hates injustice of every kind.

"He's such a little kid," said Dicky, and of course H. O. said he wasn't a little kid, and it very nearly came to being a row between them. But Oswald knows when to be generous; so he said—

"Look here! I'll pay sixpence of the scissors, and H. O. shall pay the rest, to teach him to be careful."

H. O. agreed: he is not at all a mean kid, but I found out afterwards that Alice paid his share out of her own money.

Then we wanted some new paints, and Noël wanted a pencil and a halfpenny account-book to write poetry with, and it does seem hard never to have any apples. So, somehow or other nearly all the money got spent, and we agreed that we must let the advertisement run loose a little longer.

"I only hope," Alice said, "that they won't have got all the ladies and gentlemen they want before we have got the money to write for the sample and instructions."

And I was a little afraid myself, because it seemed such a splendid chance; but we looked in the paper every day, and the advertisement was always there, so we thought it was all right.

Then we had the detective try-on—and it proved no go; and then, when all the money was gone, except a halfpenny of mine and twopence of Noël's and threepence of Dicky's and a few pennies that the girls had left, we held another council.

Dora was sewing the buttons on H. O.'s Sunday things. He got himself a knife with his money, and he cut every single one of his best buttons off. You've no idea how many buttons there are on a suit. Dora counted them. There are twenty-four, counting the little ones on the sleeves that don't undo.

Alice was trying to teach Pincher to beg; but he has too much sense when he knows you've got nothing in your hands, and the rest of us were roasting potatoes under the fire. We had made a fire on purpose, though it was rather warm. They are very good if you cut away the burnt parts —but you ought to wash them first, or you are a dirty boy.

"Well, what can we do?" said Dicky. "You are so fond of saying 'Let's do something!' and never saying what."

"We can't try the advertisement yet. Shall we try rescuing some one?" said Oswald. It was his own idea, but he didn't insist on doing it, though he is next to the eldest, for he knows it is bad manners to make people do what you want, when they would rather not.

"What was Noël's plan?" Alice asked.

"A Princess or a poetry book," said Noël sleepily. He was lying on his back on the sofa, kicking his legs. "Only I shall look for the Princess all by myself. But I'll let you see her when we're married."

"Have you got enough poetry to make a book?" Dicky asked that, and it was rather sensible of him, because when Noël came to look there were only seven of his poems that any of us could understand. There was the "Wreck of the *Malabar*," and the poem he wrote when Eliza took us to hear the Reviving Preacher, and everybody cried, and Father said it must have been the Preacher's Eloquence.

So Noël wrote—

> Oh Eloquence and what art thou?
> Ay what are thou? because we cried
> And everybody cried inside
> When they came out their eyes were red—
> And it was your doing Father said.

But Noël told Alice he got the first line and a half from a book a boy at school was going to write when he had time. Besides this there were the "Lines on a Dead Black Beetle that was poisoned":

> Oh Beetle how I weep to see
>   Thee lying on thy poor back!
> It is so very sad indeed.
>   You were so shiny and black.
> I wish you were alive again

But Eliza says wishing it is nonsense and a shame.

It was very good beetle poison, and there were hundreds of them lying dead—but Noël only wrote a piece of poetry for one of them. He said he hadn't time to do them all, and the worst of it was he didn't know which one he'd written

"There's poetry in newspapers," said Alice

it to—so Alice couldn't bury the beetle and put the lines on its grave, though she wanted to very much.

Well, it was quite plain that there wasn't enough poetry for a book.

"We might wait a year or two," said Noël. "I shall be sure to make some more some time. I thought of a piece about a fly this morning that knew condensed milk was sticky."

"But we want the money *now*," said Dicky, "and you can go on writing just the same. It will come in some time or other."

"There's poetry in newspapers," said Alice. "Down, Pincher! you'll never be a clever dog, so it's no good trying."

"Do they pay for it?" Dicky thought of that; he often thinks of things that are really important, even if they are a little dull.

"I don't know. But I shouldn't think any one would let them print their poetry without. I wouldn't I know." That was Dora; but Noël said he wouldn't mind if he didn't get paid, so long as he saw his poetry printed and his name at the end.

"We might try, anyway," said Oswald. He is always willing to give other people's ideas a fair trial.

So we copied out "The Wreck of the *Malabar*" and the other six poems on drawing-paper—Dora did it, she writes best—and Oswald drew a picture of the *Malabar* going down with all hands. It was a full-rigged schooner, and all the ropes and sails were correct; because my cousin is in the Navy, and he showed me.

We thought a long time whether we'd write a letter and send it by post with the poetry—and Dora thought it would be best. But Noël said he couldn't bear not to know at once if the paper would print the poetry, so we decided to take it.

I went with Noël, because I am the eldest, and he is not old enough to go to London by himself. Dicky said poetry was rot—and he was glad he hadn't got to make a fool of himself: that was because there was not enough money for him to go with us. H. O. couldn't come either, but he came to the station to see us off, and waved his cap and called out "Good hunting!" as the train started.

There was a lady in spectacles in the corner. She was writing with a pencil on the edges of long strips of paper that had print all down them.

When the train started she asked—

"What was that he said?"

So Oswald answered—

"It was 'Good hunting'—it's out of the Jungle book!"

"That's very pleasant to hear," the lady said; "I am very pleased to meet people who know their Jungle book. And where are you off to—the Zoological Gardens to look for Bagheera?"

We were pleased, too, to meet some one who knew the Jungle book.

So Oswald said—

"We are going to restore the fallen fortunes of the House of Bastable—and we have all thought of different ways—and we're going to try them all. Noël's way is poetry. I suppose great poets get paid?"

The lady laughed—she was awfully jolly—and said she was a sort of poet, too, and the long strips of paper were the proofs of her new book of stories. Because before a book is made into a real book with pages and a cover, they sometimes print it all on strips of paper, and the writer makes marks on it with a pencil to show the printers what idiots they are not to understand what a writer means to have printed.

We told her all about digging for treasure, and what we

meant to do. Then she asked to see Noël's poetry—and he said he didn't like—so she said, "Look here—if you'll show me yours I'll show you some of mine." So he agreed.

The jolly lady read Noël's poetry, and she said she liked it very much. And she thought a great deal of the picture of the *Malabar*. And then she said, "I write serious poetry like yours myself, too, but I have a piece here that I think you will like because it's about a boy." She gave it to us— and so I can copy it down, and I will, for it shows that some grown-up ladies are not so silly as others. I like it better than Noël's poetry, though I told him I did not, because he looked as if he was going to cry. This was very wrong, for you should always speak the truth, however unhappy it makes people. And I generally do. But I did not want him crying in the railway carriage.

The lady's piece of poetry:

> Oh when I wake up in my bed
> And see the sun all fat and red,
> I'm glad to have another day
> For all my different kinds of play.
>
> There are so many things to do—
> The things that make a man of you,
> If grown-ups did not get so vexed
> And wonder what you will do next.
>
> I often wonder whether they
> Ever made up our kinds of play—
> If they were always good as gold
> And only did what they were told.
>
> They like you best to play with tops
> And toys in boxes, bought in shops;
> They do not even know the names
> Of really interesting games,

They will not let you play with fire
Or trip your sisters up with wire,
They grudge the tea-tray for a drum,
Or booby-traps when callers come.

They don't like fishing, and it's true
You sometimes soak a suit or two:
They look on fireworks, though they're dry,
With quite a disapproving eye.

They do not understand the way
To get the most out of your day:
They do not know how hunger feels
Nor what you need between your meals.

And when you're sent to bed at night
They're happy, but they're not polite,
For through the door you hear them say:
"*He's* done *his* mischief for the day!"

She told us a lot of other pieces but I cannot remember
them, and she talked to us all the way up, and when we got
nearly to Cannon Street she said—

"I've got two new shillings here! Do you think they would
help to smooth the path to Fame?"

Noël said, "Thank you," and was going to take the shilling. But Oswald, who always remembers what he is told,
said—

"Thank you very much, but Father told us we ought
never to take anything from strangers."

"That's a nasty one," said the lady—she didn't talk a bit
like a real lady, but more like a jolly sort of grown-up boy
in a dress and hat—"a very nasty one! But don't you think
as Noël and I are both poets I might be considered a sort of
relation? You've heard of brother poets, haven't you? Don't

you think Noël and I are aunt and nephew poets, or some relationship of that kind?"

I didn't know what to say, and she went on—

"It's awfully straight of you to stick to what your Father tells you, but look here, you take the shillings, and here's my card. When you get home tell your Father all about it, and if he says No, you can just bring the shillings back to me."

So we took the shillings, and she shook hands with us and said, "Good-bye, and good hunting!"

We did tell Father about it, and he said it was all right, and when he looked at the card he told us we were highly honoured, for the lady wrote better poetry than any other lady alive now. We had never heard of her, and she seemed much too jolly for a poet. Good old Kipling! We owe him those two shillings, as well as the Jungle books!

CHAPTER V

THE POET AND THE EDITOR

IT WAS not bad sport—being in London entirely on our own hook. We asked the way to Fleet Street, where Father says all the newspaper offices are. They said straight on down Ludgate Hill—but it turned out to be quite another way. At least *we* didn't go straight on.

We got to St. Paul's. Noël would go in, and we saw where Gordon was buried—at least the monument. It is very flat, considering what a man he was.

When we came out we walked a long way, and when we asked a policeman he said we'd better go back through Smithfield. So we did. They don't burn people any more there now, so it was rather dull, besides being a long way, and Noël got very tired. He's a peaky little chap; it comes of being a poet, I think. We had a bun or two at different shops—out of the shillings—and it was quite late in the afternoon when we got to Fleet Street. The gas was lighted and the electric lights. There is a jolly Bovril sign that comes off and on in different coloured lamps. We went to the *Daily Recorder* office, and asked to see the Editor. It is a big office, very bright, with brass and mahogany and electric lights.

They told us the Editor wasn't there, but at another office. So we went down a dirty street, to a very dull-looking place. There was a man there inside, in a glass case, as if he was a museum, and he told us to write down our names and our business. So Oswald wrote—

OSWALD BASTABLE
NOËL BASTABLE
Business very private indeed

Then we waited on the stone stairs; it was very draughty. And the man in the glass case looked at us as if we were the museum instead of him. We waited a long time, and then a boy came down and said—

"The Editor can't see you. Will you please write your business?" And he laughed. I wanted to punch his head.

But Noël said, "Yes, I'll write it if you'll give me a pen and ink, and a sheet of paper and an envelope."

The boy said he'd better write by post. But Noël is a bit pig-headed; it's his worst fault. So he said—

"No, I'll write it *now*." So I backed him up by saying—

"Look at the price penny stamps are since the coal strike!"

So the boy grinned, and the man in the glass case gave us pen and paper, and Noël wrote. Oswald writes better than he does; but Noël would do it; and it took a very long time, and then it was inky.

"DEAR MR. EDITOR,—I want you to print my poetry and pay for it, and I am a friend of Mrs. Leslie's; she is a poet too.

"Your affectionate friend,
"NOËL BASTABLE."

He licked the envelope a good deal, so that that boy shouldn't read it going upstairs; and he wrote "Very private" outside, and gave the letter to the boy. I thought it wasn't any good; but in a minute the grinning boy came back, and he was quite respectful, and said—

"The Editor says, please will you step up?"

We stepped up. There were a lot of stairs and passages, and a queer sort of humming, hammering sound and a very funny smell. The boy was now very polite, and said it was the ink we smelt, and the noise was the printing machines.

After going through a lot of cold passages we came to a

door; the boy opened it, and let us go in. There was a large room, with a big, soft, blue-and-red carpet, and a roaring fire, though it was only October; and a large table with drawers, and littered with papers, just like the one in Father's study. A gentleman was sitting at one side of the table; he had a light moustache and light eyes, and he looked very young to be an editor—not nearly so old as Father. He looked very tired and sleepy, as if he had got up very early in the morning; but he was kind, and we liked him. Oswald thought he looked clever. Oswald is considered a judge of faces.

"Well," said he, "so you are Mrs. Leslie's friends?"

"I think so," said Noël; "at least she gave us each a shilling, and she wished us 'good hunting!'"

"Good hunting, eh? Well, what about this poetry of yours? Which is the poet?"

I can't think how he could have asked! Oswald is said to be a very manly-looking boy for his age. However, I thought it would look duffing to be offended, so I said—

"This is my brother Noël. He is the poet."

Noël had turned quite pale. He is disgustingly like a girl in some ways. The Editor told us to sit down, and he took the poems from Noël, and began to read them. Noël got paler and paler; I really thought he was going to faint, like he did when I held his hand under the cold-water tap, after I had accidentally cut him with my chisel. When the Editor had read the first poem—it was the one about the beetle—he got up and stood with his back to us. It was not manners; but Noël thinks he did it "to conceal his emotion," as they do in books.

He read all the poems, and then he said—

"I like your poetry very much, young man. I'll give you—let me see; how much shall I give you for it?"

"As much as ever you can," said Noël. "You see I want

a good deal of money to restore the fallen fortunes of the house of Bastable."

The gentleman put on some eye-glasses and looked hard at us. Then he sat down.

"That's a good idea," said he. "Tell me how you came to think of it. And I say, have you had any tea? They've just sent out for mine."

He rang a tingly bell, and the boy brought in a tray with a teapot and a thick cup and saucer and things, and he had to fetch another tray for us, when he was told to; and we had tea with the Editor of the *Daily Recorder*. I suppose it was a very proud moment for Noël, though I did not think of that till afterwards. The Editor asked us a lot if questions, and we told him a good deal, though of course I did not tell a stranger all our reasons for thinking that the family fortunes wanted restoring. We stayed about half an hour, and when we were going away he said again—

"I shall print all your poems, my poet; and now what do you think they're worth?"

"I don't know," Noël said. "You see I didn't write them to sell."

"Why did you write them then?" he asked.

Noël said he didn't know; he supposed because he wanted to.

"Art for Art's sake, eh?" said the Editor, and he seemed quite delighted, as though Noël had said something clever.

"Well, would a guinea meet your views?" he asked.

I have read of people being at a loss for words, and dumb with emotion, and I've read of people being turned to stone with astonishment, or joy, or something, but I never knew how silly it looked till I saw Noël standing staring at the Editor with his mouth open. He went red and he went white, and then he got crimson, as if you were rubbing more

"Well, would a guinea meet your views?" he asked

and more crimson lake on a palette. But he didn't say a word, so Oswald had to say—

"I should jolly well think so."

So the Editor gave Noël a sovereign and a shilling, and he shook hands with us both, but he thumped Noël on the back and said—

"Buck up, old man! It's your first guinea, but it won't be your last. Now go along home, and in about ten years you can bring me some more poetry. Not before—see? I'm just taking this poetry of yours because I like it very much; but we don't put poetry in this paper at all. I shall have to put it in another paper I know of."

"What *do* you put in your paper?" I asked, for Father always takes the *Daily Chronicle*, and I didn't know what the *Recorder* was like. We chose it because it has such a glorious office, and a clock outside lighted up.

"Oh, news," said he, "and dull articles, and things about Celebrities. If you knew any Celebrities, now?"

Noël asked him what Celebrities were.

"Oh, the Queen and the Princes, and people with titles, and people who write, or sing, or act—or do something clever or wicked."

"I don't know anybody wicked," said Oswald, wishing he had known Dick Turpin, or Claude Duval, so as to be able to tell the Editor things about them. "But I know some one with a title—Lord Tottenham."

"The mad old Protectionist, eh? How did you come to know him?"

"We don't know him to speak to. But he goes over the Heath every day at three, and he strides along like a giant— with a black cloak like Lord Tennyson's flying behind him, and he talks to himself like one o'clock."

"What does he say?" The Editor had sat down again, and he was fiddling with a blue pencil.

"We only heard him once, close enough to understand, and then he said, 'The curse of the country, sir—ruin and desolation!' And then he went striding along again, hitting at the furze-bushes as if they were the heads of his enemies."

"Excellent descriptive touch," said the Editor. "Well, go on."

"That's all I know about him, except that he stops in the middle of the Heath every day, and he looks all round to see if there's any one about; and if there isn't, he takes his collar off."

The Editor interrupted—which is considered rude—and said—

"You're not romancing?"

"I beg your pardon?" said Oswald.

"Drawing the long bow, I mean," said the Editor.

Oswald drew himself up, and said he wasn't a liar.

The Editor only laughed, and said romancing and lying were not at all the same; only it was important to know what you were playing at. So Oswald accepted his apology, and went on.

"We were hiding among the furze-bushes one day, and we saw him do it. He took off his collar, and he put on a clean one, and he threw the other among the furze-bushes. We picked it up afterwards, and it was a beastly paper one!"

"Thank you," said the Editor, and he got up and put his hand in his pocket. "That's well worth five shillings, and here they are. Would you like to see round the printing offices before you go home?"

I pocketed my five bob, and thanked him, and I said we should like it very much. He called another gentleman and said something we couldn't hear. Then he said good-bye again; and all this time Noël hadn't said a word. But now he said, "I've made a poem about you. It is called 'Lines to a Noble Editor.' Shall I write it down?"

The Editor gave him the blue pencil, and he sat down at the Editor's table and wrote. It was this, he told me afterwards as well as he could remember—

> May Life's choicest blessings be your lot
>   I think you ought to be very blest
> For you are going to print my poems—
>   And you may have this one as well as the rest.

"Thank you," said the Editor. "I don't think I ever had a poem addressed to me before. I shall treasure it, I assure you."

Then the other gentleman said something about Mæcenas, and we went off to see the printing office with at least one pound seven in our pockets.

It *was* good hunting, and no mistake!

But he never put Noël's poetry in the *Daily Recorder*. It was quite a long time afterwards we saw a sort of story thing in a magazine, on the station bookstall, and that kind, sleepy-looking Editor had written it, I suppose. It was not at all amusing. It said a lot about Noël and me, describing us all wrong, and saying how we had tea with the Editor; and all Noël's poems were in the story thing. I think myself the Editor seemed to make game of them, but Noël was quite pleased to see them printed—so that's all right.

It wasn't my poetry anyhow, I am glad to say.

CHAPTER VI

NOËL'S PRINCESS

SHE HAPPENED quite accidentally. We were not looking for a Princess at all just then; but Noël had said he was going to find a Princess all by himself, and marry her—and he really did. Which was rather odd, because when people say things are going to befall, very often they don't. It was different, of course, with the prophets of old.

We did not get any treasure by it, except twelve chocolate drops; but we might have done, and it was an adventure, anyhow.

Greenwich Park is a jolly good place to play in, especially the parts that aren't near Greenwich. The parts near the Heath are first-rate. I often wish the Park was nearer our house; but I suppose a Park is a difficult thing to move.

Sometimes we get Eliza to put lunch in a basket, and we go up to the Park. She likes that—it saves cooking dinner for us; and sometimes she says of her own accord, "I've made some pasties for you, and you might as well go into the Park as not. It's a lovely day."

She always tells us to rinse out the cup at the drinking-fountain, and the girls do; but I always put my head under the tap and drink. Then you are an intrepid hunter at a mountain stream—and besides, you're sure it's clean. Dicky does the same, and so does H. O. But Noël always drinks out of the cup. He says it is a golden goblet, wrought by enchanted gnomes.

The day the Princess happened was a fine hot day, last October, and we were quite tired with the walk up to the Park.

We always go in by the little gate at the top of Croom's Hill. It is the postern gate that things always happen at in stories. It was dusty walking, but when we got in the Park it was ripping, so we rested a bit, and lay on our backs, and looked up at the trees, and wished we could play monkeys. I have done it before now, but the Park-keeper makes a row if he catches you.

When we'd rested a little, Alice said—

"It was a long way to the enchanted wood, but it is very nice now we are there. I wonder what we shall find in it?"

"We shall find deer," said Dicky, "if we go to look; but they go on the other side of the Park because of the people with buns."

Saying buns made us think of lunch, so we had it; and when we had done we scratched a hole under a tree and buried the papers, because we know it spoils pretty places to leave beastly, greasy papers lying about. I remember Mother teaching me and Dora that, when we were quite little. I wish everybody's parents would teach them this useful lesson, and the same about orange peel.

When we'd eaten everything there was, Alice whispered—

"I see the white witch bear yonder among the trees! Let's track it and slay it in its lair."

"I am the bear," said Noël; so he crept away, and we followed him among the trees. Often the witch bear was out of sight, and then you didn't know where it would jump out from; but sometimes we saw it, and just followed.

"When we catch it there'll be a great fight," said Oswald; "and I shall be Count Folko of Mont Faucon."

"I'll be Gabrielle," said Dora. She is the only one of us who likes doing girl's parts.

"I'll be Sintram," said Alice; "and H. O. can be the Little Master."

"What about Dicky?"

"Oh, I can be the Pilgrim with the bones."

"Hist!" whispered Alice. "See his white fairy fur gleaming amid yonder covert!"

And I saw a bit of white too. It was Noël's collar, and it had come undone at the back.

We hunted the bear in and out of the trees, and then we lost him altogether; and suddenly we found the wall of the Park—in a place where I'm sure there wasn't a wall before. Noël wasn't anywhere about, and there was a door in the wall. And it was open; so we went through.

"The bear has hidden himself in these mountain fast-nesses," Oswald said. "I will draw my good sword and after him."

So I drew the umbrella, which Dora always will bring in case it rains, because Noël gets a cold on the chest at the least thing—and we went on.

The other side of the wall it was a stable yard, all cobble-stones. There was nobody about—but we could hear a man rubbing down a horse and hissing in the stable; so we crept very quietly past, and Alice whispered—

"'Tis the lair of the Monster Serpent; I hear his deadly hiss! Beware! Courage and despatch!"

We went over the stones on tiptoe, and we found another wall with another door in it on the other side. We went through that too, on tiptoe. It really was an adventure. And there we were in a shrubbery, and we saw something white through the trees. Dora said it was the white bear. That is so like Dora. She always begins to take part in a play just when the rest of us are getting tired of it. I don't mean this un-kindly, because I am very fond of Dora. I cannot forget how kind she was when I had bronchitis; and ingratitude is a dreadful vice. But it is quite true.

"It is not a bear," said Oswald; and we all went on, still on tiptoe, round a twisty path and on to a lawn, and there was

The funniest little girl you ever saw

Noël. His collar had come undone, as I said, and he had an inky mark on his face that he made just before we left the house, and he wouldn't let Dora wash it off, and one of his boot-laces was coming down. He was standing looking at a little girl; she was the funniest little girl you ever saw.

She was like a china doll—the sixpenny kind; she had a white face, and long yellow hair, done up very tight in two pigtails; her forehead was very big and lumpy, and her cheeks came high up, like little shelves under her eyes. Her eyes were small and blue. She had on a funny black frock, with curly braid on it, and button boots, that went almost up to her knees. Her legs were very thin. She was sitting in a hammock chair nursing a blue kitten—not a sky-blue one, of course, but the colour of a new slate pencil. As we came up we heard her say to Noël—

"Who are you?"

Noël had forgotten about the bear, and he was taking his favourite part, so he said—

"I'm Prince Camaralzaman."

The funny little girl looked pleased—

"I thought at first you were a common boy," she said. Then she saw the rest of us and said—

"Are you all Princesses and Princes too?"

Of course we said "Yes," and she said—

"I am a Princess also." She said it very well too, exactly as if it were true. We were very glad, because it is so seldom you meet any children who can begin to play right off without having everything explained to them. And even then they will say they are going to "pretend to be" a lion, or a witch, or a king. Now this little girl just said "I *am* a Princess." Then she looked at Oswald and said, "I fancy I've seen you at Baden."

Of course Oswald said, "Very likely."

The little girl had a funny voice, and all her words were quite plain, each word by itself; she didn't talk at all like we do.

H. O. asked her what the cat's name was, and she said "Katinka." Then Dicky said—

"Let's get away from the windows; if you play near windows some one inside generally knocks at them and says 'Don't.'"

The Princess put down the cat very carefully, and said—

"I am forbidden to walk off the grass."

"That's a pity," said Dora.

"But I will if you like," said the Princess.

"You mustn't do things you are forbidden to do," Dora said; but Dicky showed us that there was some more grass beyond the shrubs with only a gravel path between. So I lifted the Princess over the gravel, so that she should be able to say she hadn't walked off the grass. When we got to the other grass we all sat down, and the Princess asked us if we liked "dragées" (I know that's how you spell it, for I asked Albert-next-door's uncle).

We said we thought not, but she pulled a real silver box out of her pocket and showed us; they were just flat, round chocolates. We had two each. Then we asked her her name, and she began, and when she began she went on, and on, and on, till I thought she was never going to stop. H. O. said she had fifty names, but Dicky is very good at figures, and he says there were only eighteen. The first were Pauline, Alexandra, Alice, and Mary was one, and Victoria, for we all heard that, and it ended up with Hildegarde Cunigonde something or other, Princess of something else.

When she'd done, H. O. said, "That's jolly good! Say it again!" and she did, but even then we couldn't remember it. We told her our names, but she thought they were too short, so when it was Noël's turn he said he was Prince Noël

Camaralzaman Ivan Constantine Charlemagne James John Edward Biggs Maximilian Bastable Prince of Lewisham, but when she asked him to say it again of course he could only get the first two names right, because he'd made it up as he went on.

So the Princess said, "You are quite old enough to know your own name." She was very grave and serious.

She told us that she was the fifth cousin of Queen Victoria. We asked who the other cousins were, but she did not seem to understand. She went on and said she was seven times removed. She couldn't tell us what that meant either, but Oswald thinks it means that the Queen's cousins are so fond of her that they will keep coming bothering, so the Queen's servants have orders to remove them. This little girl must have been very fond of the Queen to try so often to see her and to have been seven times removed. We could see that it is considered something to be proud of, but we thought it was hard on the Queen that her cousins wouldn't let her alone.

Presently the little girl asked us where our maids and governesses were.

We told her we hadn't any just now. And she said—

"How pleasant! And did you come here alone?"

"Yes," said Dora; "we came across the Heath."

"You are very fortunate," said the little girl. She sat very upright on the grass, with her fat little hands in her lap. "I should like to go on the Heath. There are donkeys there, with white saddle covers. I should like to ride them, but my governess will not permit it."

"I'm glad we haven't a governess," H. O. said. "We ride the donkeys whenever we have any pennies, and once I gave the man another penny to make it gallop."

"You are indeed fortunate!" said the Princess again, and when she looked sad the shelves on her cheeks showed more

She sat very upright on the grass, with her fat little hands in her lap

than ever. You could have laid a sixpence on them quite
safely if you had had one.

"Never mind," said Noël; "I've got a lot of money. Come
out and have a ride now." But the little girl shook her head
and said she was afraid it would not be correct.

Dora said she was quite right; then all of a sudden came
one of those uncomfortable times when nobody can think of
anything to say, so we sat and looked at each other. But at
last Alice said we ought to be going.

"Do not go yet," the little girl said. "At what time did they
order your carriage?"

"Our carriage is a fairy one, drawn by griffins, and it
comes when we wish for it," said Noël.

The little girl looked at him very queerly, and said, "That
is out of a picture-book."

Then Noël said he thought it was about time he was
married if we were to be home in time for tea. The little girl
was rather stupid over it, but she did what we told her, and
we married them with Dora's pocket-handkerchief for a
veil, and the ring off the back of one of the buttons on
H. O.'s blouse just went on her little finger.

Then we showed her how to play cross-touch, and puss
in the corner, and tag. It was funny, she didn't know any
games but battledore and shuttlecock and *les graces*. But
she really began to laugh at last and not to look quite so like
a doll.

She was Puss and was running after Dicky when suddenly
she stopped short and looked as if she was going to cry. And
we looked too, and there were two prim ladies with little
mouths and tight hair. One of them said in quite an awful
voice, "Pauline, who are these children?" and her voice was
gruff, with very curly R's.

The little girl said we were Princes and Princesses—which

was silly, to a grown-up person that is not a great friend of yours.

The gruff lady gave a short, horrid laugh, like a husky bark, and said—

"Princes, indeed! They're only common children."

Dora turned very red and began to speak, but the little girl cried out "Common children! Oh, I am so glad! When I am grown up I'll always play with common children."

And she ran at us, and began to kiss us one by one, beginning with Alice; she had got to H. O. when the horrid lady said—

"Your Highness—go indoors at once!"

The little girl answered, "I won't!" Then the prim lady said—

"Wilson, carry her Highness indoors."

And the little girl was carried away screaming and kicking with her little thin legs and her buttoned boots, and between her screams she shrieked: "Common children! I am glad, glad, glad! Common children! Common children!"

The nasty lady then remarked—

"Go at once, or I will send for the police!"

So we went. H. O. made a face at her and so did Alice but Oswald took off his cap and said he was sorry if she was annoyed about anything; for Oswald has always been taught to be polite to ladies, however nasty. Dicky took his off, too, when he saw me do it; he says he did it first, but that is a mistake. If I were really a common boy I should say it was a lie.

Then we all came away, and when we got outside Dora said, "So she was really a Princess. Fancy a Princess living *there!*"

"Even Princesses have to live somewhere," said Dicky.

"And I thought it was play. And it was real. I wish I'd

The little girl was carried away
screaming

known! I should have liked to ask her lots of things," said Alice.

H. O. said he would have liked to ask her what she had for dinner and whether she had a crown.

I felt, myself, we had lost a chance of finding out a great deal about kings and queens. I might have known such a stupid-looking little girl would never have been able to pretend as well as that.

So we all went home across the Heath, and made dripping toast for tea.

When we were eating it Noël said, "I wish I could give *her* some! It is very good."

He sighed as he said it, and his mouth was very full, so we knew he was thinking of his Princess. He says now that she was as beautiful as the day, but we remember her quite well, and she was nothing of the kind.

CHAPTER VII

BEING BANDITS

NOËL WAS quite tiresome for ever so long after we found the Princess. He would keep on wanting to go to the Park when the rest of us didn't, and though we went several times to please him, we never found that door open again, and all of us except him knew from the first that it would be no go.

So now we thought it was time to do something to rouse him from the stupor of despair, which is always done to heroes when anything baffling has occurred. Besides, we were getting very short of money again—the fortunes of your house cannot be restored (not so that they will last, that is), even by the one pound eight we got when we had the "good hunting." We spent a good deal of that on presents for Father's birthday. We got him a paper-weight, like a glass bun, with a picture of Lewisham Church at the bottom; and a blotting-pad, and a box of preserved fruits, and an ivory penholder with a view of Greenwich Park in the little hole where you look through at the top. He was most awfully pleased and surprised, and when he heard how Noël and Oswald had earned the money to buy the things he was more surprised still. Nearly all the rest of our money went to get fireworks for the Fifth of November. We got six Catherine wheels and four rockets; two hand-lights, one red and one green; a sixpenny maroon; two Roman-candles —they cost a shilling; some Italian streamers, a fairy fountain, and a tourbillon that cost eighteen-pence and was very nearly worth it.

But I think crackers and squibs are a mistake. It's true you get a lot of them for the money, and they are not bad fun for the first two or three dozen, but you get jolly sick of them before you've let off your sixpenn'orth. And the only amusing way is not allowed: it is putting them in the fire.

It always seems a long time till the evening when you have got fireworks in the house, and I think as it was a rather foggy day we should have decided to let them off directly after breakfast, only Father had said he would help us to let them off at eight o'clock after he had had his dinner, and you ought never to disappoint your father if you can help it.

You see we had three good reasons for trying H. O.'s idea of restoring the fallen fortunes of our house by becoming bandits on the Fifth of November. We had a fourth reason as well, and that was the best reason of the lot. You remember Dora thought it would be wrong to be bandits. And the Fifth of November came while Dora was away at Stroud staying with her godmother. Stroud is in Gloucestershire. We were determined to do it while she was out of the way, because we did not think it wrong, and besides we meant to do it anyhow.

We held a Council, of course, and laid our plans very carefully. We let H. O. be Captain, because it was his idea. Oswald was Lieutenant. Oswald was quite fair, because he let H. O. call himself Captain; but Oswald is the eldest next to Dora, after all.

Our plan was this. We were all to go up on to the Heath. Our house is in the Lewisham Road, but it's quite close to the Heath if you cut up the short way opposite the confectioner's, past the nursery gardens and the cottage hospital, and turn to the left again and afterwards to the right. You come out then at the top of the hill, where the big guns are with the iron fence round them, and where the bands play on Thursday evenings in the summer.

We were to lurk in ambush there, and waylay an unwary traveller. We were to call upon him to surrender his arms, and then bring him home and put him in the deepest dungeon below the castle moat; then we were to load him with chains and send to his friends for ransom. You may think we had no chains, but you are wrong, because we used to keep two other dogs once, besides Pincher, before the fall of the fortunes of the ancient House of Bastable. And they were quite big dogs.

It was latish in the afternoon before we started. We thought we could lurk better if it was nearly dark. It was rather foggy, and we waited a good while beside the railings, but all the belated travellers were either grown up or else they were Board School children. We weren't going to get into a row with grown-up people—especially strangers— and no true bandit would ever stoop to ask a ransom from the relations of the poor and needy. So we thought it better to wait.

As I said, it was Guy Fawkes' Day, and if it had not been we should never have been able to be bandits at all, for the unwary traveller we did catch had been forbidden to go out because he had a cold in his head. But he would run out to follow a guy, without even putting on a coat or a comforter, and it was a very damp, foggy afternoon and nearly dark, so you see it was his own fault entirely, and served him jolly well right.

We saw him coming over the Heath just as we were deciding to go home to tea. He had followed the guy right across to the village (we call Blackheath the village; I don't know why), and he was coming back dragging his feet and sniffing.

"Hist, an unwary traveller approaches!" whispered Oswald.

"Muffle your horses' heads and see to the priming of your pistols," muttered Alice. She always will play boys' parts, and she makes Ellis cut her hair short on purpose. Ellis is a very obliging hairdresser.

"Steal softly upon him," said Noël; "for lo! 'tis dusk, and no human eyes can mark our deeds."

So we ran out and surrounded the unwary traveller. It turned out to be Albert-next-door, and he was very frightened indeed until he saw who we were.

"Surrender!" hissed Oswald, in a desperate-sounding voice, as he caught the arm of the Unwary. And Albert-next-door said, "All right! I'm surrendering as hard as I can. You needn't pull my arm off."

We explained to him that resistance was useless, and I think he saw that from the first. We held him tight by both arms, and we marched him home down the hill in a hollow square of five.

He wanted to tell us about the guy, but we made him see that it was not proper for prisoners to talk to the guard, especially about guys that the prisoner had been told not to go after because of his cold.

When we got to where we live he said, "All right, I don't want to tell you. You'll wish I had afterwards. You never saw such a guy."

"I can see *you!*" said H. O. It was very rude, and Oswald told him so at once, because it is his duty as an elder brother. But H. O. is very young and does not know better yet, and besides it wasn't bad for H. O.

Albert-next-door said, "You haven't any manners, and I want to go in to my tea. Let go of me!"

But Alice told him, quite kindly, that he was not going in to his tea, but coming with us.

"I'm not," said Albert-next-door; "I'm going home. Leave go! I've got a bad cold. You're making it worse." Then he tried to cough, which was very silly, because we'd seen him in the morning, and he'd told us where the cold was that he wasn't to go out with. When he had tried to cough, he said, "Leave go of me! You see my cold's getting worse."

"You should have thought of that before," said Dicky; "you're coming in with us."

"Don't be silly," said Noël; "you know we told you at the very beginning that resistance was useless. There is no disgrace in yielding. We are five to your one."

By this time Eliza had opened the door, and we thought it best to take him in without any more parleying. To parley with a prisoner is not done by bandits.

Directly we got him safe into the nursery, H. O. began to jump about and say, "Now you're a prisoner really and truly!"

And Albert-next-door began to cry. He always does. I wonder he didn't begin long before—but Alice fetched him one of the dried fruits we gave Father for his birthday. It was a green walnut. I have noticed the walnuts and the plums always get left till the last in the box: the apricots go first, and then the figs and pears; and the cherries, if there are any.

So he ate it and shut up. Then we explained his position to him, so that there should be no mistake, and he couldn't say afterwards that he had not understood.

"There will be no violence," said Oswald—he was now Captain of the Bandits, because we all know H. O. likes to be Chaplain when we play prisoners—"no violence. But you will be confined in a dark, subterranean dungeon where toads and snakes crawl, and but little of the light of day filters through the heavily mullioned windows. You will be loaded with chains. Now don't begin again, Baby, there's nothing to cry about; straw will be your pallet; beside you the gaoler will set a ewer—a ewer is only a jug, stupid; it won't eat you—a ewer with water; and a mouldering crust will be your food."

But Albert-next-door never enters into the spirit of the thing. He mumbled something about tea-time.

Now Oswald, though stern, is always just, and besides we were all rather hungry, and tea was ready. So we had it at once, Albert-next-door and all—and we gave him what was left of the four-pound jar of apricot jam we got with the money Noël got for his poetry. And we saved our crusts for the prisoner.

Albert-next-door was very tiresome. Nobody could have had a nicer prison than he had. We fenced him into a corner with the old wire nursery fender and all the chairs, instead of putting him in the coal-cellar as we had first intended. And when he said the dog-chains were cold the girls were kind enough to warm his fetters thoroughly at the fire before we put them on him.

We got the straw cases of some bottles of wine some one sent Father one Christmas—it is some years ago, but the cases are quite good. We unpicked them very carefully and pulled them to pieces and scattered the straw about. It made a lovely straw pallet, and took ever so long to make—but Albert-next-door has yet to learn what gratitude really is. We got the bread trencher for the wooden platter where the prisoner's crusts were put—they were not mouldy, but we could not wait till they got so, and for the ewer we got the toilet jug out of the spare-room where nobody ever sleeps. And even then Albert-next-door couldn't be happy like the rest of us. He howled and cried and tried to get out, and he knocked the ewer over and stamped on the mouldering crusts. Luckily there was no water in the ewer because we had forgotten it, only dust and spiders. So we tied him up with the clothes-line from the back kitchen, and we had to hurry up, which was a pity for him. We might have had him rescued by a devoted page if he hadn't been so tiresome. In fact Noël was actually dressing up for the page when Albert-next-door kicked over the prison ewer.

We got a sheet of paper out of an old exercise-book, and

we made H. O. prick his own thumb, because he is our little brother and it is our duty to teach him to be brave. We none of us mind pricking ourselves; we've done it heaps of times. H. O. didn't like it, but he agreed to do it, and I helped him a little because he was so slow, and when he saw the red bead of blood getting fatter and bigger as I squeezed his thumb he was very pleased, just as I had told him he would be.

This is what we wrote with H. O.'s blood, only the blood gave out when we got to "Restored," and we had to write the rest with crimson lake, which is not the same colour, though I always use it, myself, for painting wounds.

While Oswald was writing it he heard Alice whispering to the prisoner that it would soon be over, and it was only play. The prisoner left off howling, so I pretended not to hear what she said. A Bandit Captain has to overlook things sometimes. This was the letter:

"Albert Morrison is held a prisoner by Bandits. On payment of three thousand pounds he will be restored to his sorrowing relatives, and all will be forgotten and forgiven."

I was not sure about the last part, but Dicky was certain he had seen it in the paper, so I suppose it must have been all right.

We let H. O. take the letter; it was only fair, as it was his blood it was written with, and told him to leave it next door for Mrs. Morrison.

H. O. came back quite quickly, and Albert-next-door's uncle came with him.

"What is all this, Albert?" he cried. "Alas, alas, my nephew! Do I find you the prisoner of a desperate band of brigands?"

"Bandits," said H. O., "you know it says bandits."

"I beg your pardon, gentlemen," said Albert-next-door's uncle, "bandits it is, of course. This, Albert, is the direct result of the pursuit of the guy on an occasion when your doting mother had expressly warned you to forgo the pleasures of the chase."

Albert said it wasn't his fault, and he hadn't wanted to play.

"So ho!" said his uncle, "impenitent too! Where's the dungeon?"

We explained the dungeon, and showed him the straw pallet and the ewer and the mouldering crusts and other things.

"Very pretty and complete," he said. "Albert, you are more highly privileged than ever I was. No one ever made me a nice dungeon when I was your age. I think I had better leave you where you are."

Albert began to cry again and said he was sorry, and he would be a good boy.

"And on this old familiar basis you expect me to ransom you, do you? Honestly, my nephew, I doubt whether you are worth it. Besides, the sum mentioned in this document strikes me as excessive: Albert really is *not* worth three thousand pounds. Also, by a strange and unfortunate chance I haven't the money about me. Couldn't you take less?"

We said perhaps we could.

"Say eightpence," suggested Albert-next-door's uncle, "which is all the small change I happen to have on my person."

"Thank you very much," said Alice as he held it out; "but are you sure you can spare it? Because really it was only play."

"Quite sure. Now, Albert, the game is over. You had better run home to your mother and tell her how much you've enjoyed yourself."

When Albert-next-door had gone his uncle sat in the Guy Fawkes armchair and took Alice on his knee, and we sat round the fire waiting till it would be time to let off our fireworks. We roasted the chestnuts he sent Dicky out for, and he told us stories till it was nearly seven. His stories are first-rate—he does all the parts in different voices. At last he said—

"Look here, young 'uns. I like to see you play and enjoy yourselves, and I don't think it hurts Albert to enjoy himself too."

"I don't think he did much," said H. O. But I knew what Albert-next-door's uncle meant because I am much older than H. O. He went on—

"But what about Albert's mother? Didn't you think how anxious she would be at his not coming home? As it happens I saw him come in with you, so we knew it was all right. But if I hadn't, eh?"

He only talks like that when he is very serious, or even angry. Other times he talks like people in books—to us, I mean.

We none of us said anything. But I was thinking. Then Alice spoke.

Girls seem not to mind saying things that we don't say. She put her arms round Albert-next-door's uncle's neck and said—

"We're very, very sorry. We didn't think about his mother. You see we try very hard not to think about other people's mothers because——"

Just then we heard Father's key in the door and Albert-next-door's uncle kissed Alice and put her down, and we all went down to meet Father. As we went I thought I heard Albert-next-door's uncle say something that sounded like "Poor little beggars!"

He couldn't have meant us, when we'd been having such a jolly time, and chestnuts, and fireworks to look forward to after dinner and everything!

CHAPTER VIII

BEING EDITORS

IT WAS Albert's uncle who thought of our trying a newspaper. He said he thought we should not find the bandit business a paying industry, as a permanency, and that journalism might be.

We had sold Noël's poetry and that piece of information about Lord Tottenham to the good editor, so we thought it would not be a bad idea to have a newspaper of our own. We saw plainly that editors must be very rich and powerful, because of the grand office and the man in the glass case, like a museum, and the soft carpets and big writing-table. Besides our having seen a whole handful of money that the editor pulled out quite carelessly from his trousers pocket when he gave me my five bob.

Dora wanted to be editor and so did Oswald, but he gave way to her because she is a girl, and afterwards he knew that it is true what it says in the copy-books about Virtue being its own Reward. Because you've no idea what a bother it is. Everybody wanted to put in everything just as they liked, no matter how much room there was on the page. It was simply awful! Dora put up with it as long as she could and then she said if she wasn't let alone she wouldn't go on being editor; they could be the paper's editors themselves, so there.

Then Oswald said, like a good brother: "I will help you if you like, Dora," and she said, "You're more trouble than all the rest of them! Come and be editor and see how you like it. I give it up to you." But she didn't, and we did it together. We let Albert-next-door be sub-editor, because he had hurt his foot with a nail in his boot that gathered.

When it was done Albert-next-door's uncle had it copied for us in typewriting, and we sent copies to all our friends, and then of course there was no one left that we could ask to buy it. We did not think of that until too late. We called the paper the *Lewisham Recorder;* Lewisham because we live there, and Recorder in memory of the good editor. I could write a better paper on my head, but an editor is not allowed to write all the paper. It is very hard, but he is not. You just have to fill up with what you can get from other writers. If I ever have time I will write a paper all by myself. It won't be patchy. We had no time to make it an illustrated paper, but I drew the ship going down with all hands for the first copy. But the typewriter can't draw ships, so it was left out in the other copies. The time the first paper took to write out no one would believe! This was the Newspaper:

The Lewisham Recorder

EDITORS: DORA AND OSWALD BASTABLE

Editorial Note

Every paper is written for some reason. Ours is because we want to sell it and get money. If what we have written brings happiness to any sad heart we shall not have laboured in vain. But we want the money too. Many papers are content with the sad heart and the happiness, but we are not like that, and it is best not to be deceitful. Editors.

There will be two serial stories; one by Dicky and one by all of us. In a serial story you only put in one chapter at a time. But we shall put all our serial story at once, if Dora has time to copy it. Dicky's will come later on.

SERIAL STORY

BY US ALL

CHAPTER I *By Dora*

The sun was setting behind a romantic-looking tower when two strangers might have been observed descending the crest of the hill. The elder, a man in the prime of life; the other a handsome youth who reminded everybody of Quentin Durward. They approached the Castle, in which the fair Lady Alicia awaited her deliverers. She leaned from the castellated window and waved her lily hand as they approached. They returned her signal, and retired to seek rest and refreshment at a neighbouring hostelry.

CHAPTER II *By Alice*

The Princess was very uncomfortable in the tower, because her fairy godmother had told her all sorts of horrid things would happen if she didn't catch a mouse every day, and she had caught so many mice that now there were hardly any left to catch. So she sent her carrier pigeon to ask the noble strangers if they could send her a few mice—because she would be of age in a few days and then it wouldn't matter. So the fairy godmother—— (I'm very sorry, but there's no room to make the chapters any longer. ED).

CHAPTER III *By the Sub-Editor*

(I can't—I'd much rather not—I don't know how.)

Chapter IV *By Dicky*

I must now retrace my steps and tell you something about our hero. You must know he had been to an awfully jolly school, where they had turkey and goose every day for dinner, and never any mutton, and as many helps of pudding as a fellow cared to send up his plate for—so of course they had all grown up very strong, and before he left school he challenged the Head to have it out man to man, and he gave it him, I tell you. That was the education that made him able to fight Red Indians, and to be the stranger who might have been observed in the first chapter.

Chapter V *By Noël*

I think it's time something happened in this story. So then the dragon he came out, blowing fire out of his nose, and he said—

> "Come on, you valiant man and true,
> I'd like to have a set to along of you!"

(That's bad English.—Ed. I don't care; it's what the dragon said. Who told you dragons didn't talk bad English? Noël.) So the hero, whose name was Noeloninuris, replied—

> "My blade is sharp, my axe is keen,
> You're not nearly as big as a good many
>   dragons I've seen."

(Don't put in so much poetry, Noël. It's not fair, because none of the others can do it. Ed.)

And then they went at it, and he beat the dragon, just as he did the Head in Dicky's part of the story, and so he married the Princess, and they lived——(No they didn't—not till the last chapter. ED.)

CHAPTER VI *By H.O.*

I think it's a very nice story—but what about the mice? I don't want to say any more. Dora can have what's left of my chapter.

CHAPTER VII *By the Editors*

And so when the dragon was dead there were lots of mice, because he used to kill them for his tea; but now they rapidly multiplied and ravaged the country, so the fair lady Alicia, sometimes called the princess, had to say she would not marry anyone unless they could rid the country of this plague of mice. Then the Prince, whose real name didn't begin with N, but was Osrawalddo, waved his magic sword, and the dragon stood before them, bowing gracefully. They made him promise to be good, and then they forgave him; and when the wedding breakfast came, all the bones were saved for him. And so they were married and lived happy ever after.

(What became of the other stranger? NOËL. The dragon ate him because he asked too many questions. EDITORS.)

This is the end of the story.

INSTRUCTIVE

It only takes four hours and a quarter now to get from London to Manchester; but I should not think any one would if they could help it.

A dreadful warning. A wicked boy told me a very in-structive thing about ginger. They had opened one of the large jars, and he happened to take out quite a lot, and he made it all right by dropping marbles in, till there was as much ginger as before. But he told me that on the Sunday, when it was coming near the part where there is only juice generally, I had no idea what his feelings were. I don't see what he could have said when they asked him. I should be sorry to act like it.

SCIENTIFIC

Experiments should always be made out of doors. And don't use benzoline. DICKY.

(That was when he burnt his eyebrows off. ED.)

The earth is 2,400 miles round, and 800 through—at least I think so, but perhaps it's the other way. DICKY.

(You ought to have been sure before you began. ED.)

SCIENTIFIC COLUMN

In this so-called Nineteenth Century Science is but too little considered in the nurseries of the rich and proud. But we are not like that.

It is not generally known that if you put bits of camphor in luke-warm water it will move about. If you drop sweet oil in, the camphor will dart away and then stop moving. But don't drop any till you are tired of it, because the cam-phor won't any more afterwards. Much amusement and in-struction is lost by not knowing things like this.

If you put a sixpence under a shilling in a wine-glass, and

blow hard down the side of the glass, the sixpence will jump up and sit on the top of the shilling. At least I can't do it myself, but my cousin can. He is in the Navy.

ANSWERS TO CORRESPONDENTS

Noël. You are very poetical, but I am sorry to say it will not do.

Alice. Nothing will ever make your hair curl, so it's no use. Some people say it's more important to tidy up as you go along. I don't mean you in particular, but every one.

H. O. We never said you were tubby, but the Editor does not know any cure.

Noël. If there is any of the paper over when this newspaper is finished, I will exchange it for your shut-up inkstand, or the knife that has the useful thing in it for taking stones out of horses' feet, but you can't have it without.

H. O. There are many ways how your steam engine might stop working. You might ask Dicky. He knows one of them. I think it is the way yours stopped.

Noël. If you think that by filling the garden with sand you can make crabs build their nests there you are not at all sensible.

You have altered your poem about the battle of Waterloo so often, that we cannot read it except where the Duke waves his sword and says some thing we can't read either. Why did you write it on blotting-paper with purple chalk? ED.

(Because you know who sneaked my pencil. NOËL.)

POETRY

The Assyrian came down like a wolf on the fold,
And the way he came down was awful, I'm told;

But it's nothing to the way one of the Editors comes
    down on me,
If I crumble my bread-and-butter or spill my tea.

NOËL.

CURIOUS FACTS

If you hold a guinea-pig up by his tail his eyes drop out.

You can't do half the things yourself that children in
books do, making models or so on. I wonder why?—ALICE.

If you take a date's stone out and put in an almond and
eat them together, it is prime. I found this out.—SUB-EDITOR.

If you put your wet hand into boiling lead it will not hurt
you if you draw it out quickly enough. I have never tried
this. DORA.

THE PURRING CLASS
(Instructive Article)

If I ever keep a school everything shall be quite different.
Nobody shall learn anything they don't want to. And sometimes instead of having masters and mistresses we will have
cats, and we will dress up in cat skins and learn purring.

"Now, my dears," the old cat will say, "one, two, three
—all purr together," and we shall purr like anything.

She won't teach us to mew, but we shall know how without teaching. Children do know some things without being
taught. ALICE.

POETRY
(Translated into French by Dora)
Quand j'étais jeune et j'étais fou
J'achetai un violon pour dix-huit sous
Et tous les airs que je jouai
Etait over the hills and far away.

Another piece of it

Merci jolie vache qui fait
Bon lait pour mon déjeuner
Tous les matins tous les soirs
Mon pain je mange, ton lait je boire.

RECREATIONS

It is a mistake to think that cats are playful. I often try to get a cat to play with me, and she never seems to care about the game, no matter how little it hurts.—H. O.

Making pots and pans with clay is fun, but do not tell the grown-ups. It is better to surprise them, and then you must say at once how easily it washes off—much easier than ink. DICKY.

SAM REDFERN, OR THE BUSHRANGER'S BURIAL
By Dicky

"Well, Annie, I have bad news for you," said Mr. Ridgway, as he entered the comfortable dining-room of his cabin in the Bush. "Sam Redfern the Bushranger is about this part of the Bush just now. I hope he will not attack us with his gang."

"I hope not," responded Annie, a gentle maiden of some sixteen summers.

Just then came a knock at the door of the hut, and a gruff voice asked them to open the door.

"It is Sam Redfern the Bushranger, father," said the girl.

"The same," responded the voice, and the next moment the hall door was smashed in, and Sam Redfern sprang in, followed by his gang.

Chapter II

Annie's Father was at once overpowered, and Annie herself lay bound with cords on the drawing-room sofa. Sam Redfern set a guard round the lonely hut and all human aid was despaired of. But you never know. Far away in the Bush a different scene was being enacted.

"Must be Injuns," said a tall man to himself as he pushed his way through the brushwood. It was Jim Carlton, the celebrated detective. "I know them," he added; "they are Apaches." Just then ten Indians in full war-paint appeared. Carlton raised his rifle and fired, and slinging their scalps on his arm he hastened towards the humble log hut where resided his affianced bride, Annie Ridgway, sometimes known as the Flower of the Bush.

Chapter III

The moon was low on the horizon, and Sam Redfern was seated at a drinking bout with some of his boon companions.

They had rifled the cellars of the hut, and the rich wines flowed like water in the golden goblets of Mr. Ridgway.

But Annie had made friends with one of the gang, a noble, good-hearted man who had joined Sam Redfern by mistake, and she had told him to go and get the police as quickly as possible.

"Ha! Ha!" cried Redfern, "now I am enjoying myself." He little knew that his doom was near upon him.

Just then Annie gave a piercing scream, and Sam Redfern got up, seizing his revolver.

"Who are you?" he cried, as a man entered.

"I am Jim Carlton, the celebrated detective," said the new arrival.

Sam Redfern's revolver dropped from his nerveless fingers, but the next moment he had sprung upon the detective with the well-known activity of the mountain sheep, and Annie shrieked, for she had grown to love the rough Bushranger.

(To be continued at the end of the paper if there is room)

SCHOLASTIC

A new slate is horrid till it is washed in milk. I like the green spots on them to draw patterns round. I know a good way to make a slate-pencil squeak, but I won't put it in because I don't want to make it common.—SUB-EDITOR.

Peppermint is a great help with arithmetic. The boy who was second in the Oxford Local always did it. He gave me two. The examiner said to him, "Are you eating peppermints?" And he said, "No, sir." He told me afterwards it was quite true, because he was only sucking one. I'm glad I wasn't asked. I should never have thought of that, and I should have had to say "Yes." OSWALD.

THE WRECK OF THE "MALABAR"

By Noël

(Author of "A Dream of Ancient Ancestors.") He isn't really—but he put it in to make it seem more real.

Hark! what is that noise of rolling
Waves and thunder in the air?
'Tis the death-knell of the sailors
And officers and passengers of the
good ship *Malabar*.

It was a fair and lovely noon
   When the good ship put out of port
And people said "Ah little we think
   How soon she will be the elements' sport."

She was indeed a lovely sight
   Upon the billows with sails spread
But the captain folded his gloomy arms
   Ah—if she had been a life-boat instead!

See the captain stern yet gloomy
   Flings his son upon a rock
Hoping that there his darling boy
   May escape the wreck.

Alas in vain the loud winds roared
   And nobody was saved.
That was the wreck of the *Malabar*,
   Then let us toll for the brave. NOËL.

GARDENING NOTES

It is useless to plant cherry-stones in the hope of eating the fruit, because they don't!

Alice won't lend her gardening tools again, because the last time Noël left them out in the rain, and I don't like it. He said he didn't.

SEEDS AND BULBS

These are useful to play at shop with, until you are ready. Not at dinner-parties, for they will not grow unless un-cooked. Potatoes are not grown with seed, but with chopped-up potatoes. Apple trees are grown from twigs, which is less wasteful.

Oak trees come from acorns. Every one knows this. When Noël says he could grow one from a peach stone wrapped up in oak leaves, he shows that he knows nothing about gardening but marigolds, and when I passed by his garden I thought they seemed just like weeds now the flowers have been picked.

A boy once dared me to eat a bulb.

Dogs are very industrious and fond of gardening. Pincher is always planting bones, but they never grow up. There couldn't be a bone tree. I think this is what makes him bark so unhappily at night. He has never tried planting dog-biscuit, but he is fonder of bones, and perhaps he wants to be quite sure about them first.

———

Sam Redfern, or the Bushranger's Burial
By Dick
Chapter IV and Last

This would have been a jolly good story if they had let me finish at the beginning of the paper, as I wanted to. But now I have forgotten how I meant it to end, and I have lost my book about Red Indians, and all my *Boys of England* have been sneaked. The girls say "Good riddance!" so I expect they did it. They want me just to put in which Annie married, but I shan't, so they will never know.

———

We have now put everything we can think of into the paper. It takes a lot of thinking about. I don't know how grown-ups manage to write all they do. It must make their heads ache, especially lesson books.

Albert-next-door only wrote one chapter of the serial

story, but he could have done some more if he had wanted to. He could not write out any of the things because he cannot spell. He says he can, but it takes him such a long time he might just as well not be able. There are one or two things more. I am sick of it, but Dora says she will write them in.

Legal answer wanted. A quantity of excellent string is offered if you know whether there really is a law passed about not buying gunpowder under thirteen. DICKY.

The price of this paper is one shilling each, and sixpence extra for the picture of the *Malabar* going down with all hands. If we sell one hundred copies we will write another paper.

* * * *

And so we would have done, but we never did. Albert-next-door's uncle gave us two shillings, that was all. You can't restore fallen fortunes with two shillings!

CHAPTER IX

THE G.B.

BEING EDITORS is not the best way to wealth. We all feel this now, and highwaymen are not respected any more like they used to be.

I am sure we had tried our best to restore our fallen fortunes. We felt their fall very much, because we knew the Bastables had been rich once. Dora and Oswald can remember when Father was always bringing nice things home from London, and there used to be turkeys and geese and wine and cigars come by the carrier at Christmas-time, and boxes of candied fruit and French plums in ornamental boxes with silk and velvet and gilding on them. They were called prunes, but the prunes you buy at the grocer's are quite different. But now there is seldom anything nice brought from London, and the turkey and the prune people have forgotten Father's address.

"How *can* we restore those beastly fallen fortunes?" said Oswald. "We've tried digging and writing and princesses and being editors."

"And being bandits," said H. O.

"When did you try that?" asked Dora quickly. "You know I told you it was wrong."

"It wasn't wrong the way we did it," said Alice, quicker still, before Oswald could say, "Who asked you to tell us anything about it?" which would have been rude, and he is glad he didn't. "We only caught Albert-next-door."

"Oh, Albert-next-door!" said Dora contemptuously, and I felt more comfortable; for even after I didn't say "Who asked you, and cetera," I was afraid Dora was going to come the good elder sister over us. She does that a jolly sight too often.

Dicky looked up from the paper he was reading and said, "This sounds likely," and he read out—

£100 secures partnership in lucrative business for sale of useful patent. £10 weekly. No personal attendance necessary. Jobbins, 300, Old Street Road.

"I wish we could secure that partnership," said Oswald. He is twelve, and a very thoughtful boy for his age.

Alice looked up from her painting. She was trying to paint a fairy queen's frock with green bice, and it wouldn't rub. There is something funny about green bice. It never will rub off, no matter how expensive your paint-box is—and even boiling water is very little use.

She said, "Bother the bice! And, Oswald, it's no use thinking about that. Where are we to get a hundred pounds?"

"Ten pounds a week is five pounds to us," Oswald went on—he had done the sum in his head while Alice was talking—"because partnership means halves. It would be A 1."

Noël sat sucking his pencil—he had been writing poetry as usual. I saw the first two lines—

> I wonder why Green Bice
> Is never very nice.

Suddenly he said, "I wish a fairy would come down the chimney and drop a jewel on the table—a jewel worth just a hundred pounds."

"She might as well give you the hundred pounds while she was about it," said Dora.

"Or while she was about it she might as well give us five pounds a week," said Alice.

"Or fifty," said I.

"Or five hundred," said Dicky.

I saw H. O. open his mouth, and I knew he was going to say, "Or five thousand," so I said:

"Well, she won't give us fivepence, but if you'd only do as I am always saying, and rescue a wealthy old gentleman from deadly peril he would give us a pot of money, and we could have the partnership and five pounds a week. Five pounds a week would buy a great many things."

Then Dicky said, "Why shouldn't we borrow it?"

So we said, "Who from?" and then he read this out of the paper—

MONEY PRIVATELY WITHOUT FEES
THE BOND STREET BANK
Manager, Z. Rosenbaum.

Advances cash from £20 to £10,000 on ladies' or gentlemen's note of hand alone, without security. No fees. No inquiries. Absolute privacy guaranteed.

"What does it all mean?" asked H. O.

"It means that there is a kind gentleman who has a lot of money, and he doesn't know enough poor people to help, so he puts it in the paper that he will help them, by lending them his money—that's it, isn't it, Dicky?"

Dora explained this and Dicky said, "Yes." And H. O. said he was a Generous Benefactor, like in Miss Edgeworth. Then Noël wanted to know what a note of hand was, and Dicky knew that, because he had read it in a book, and it was just a letter saying you will pay the money when you can, and signed with your name.

"No inquiries!" said Alice. "Oh—Dicky—do you think he would?"

"Yes, I think so," said Dicky. "I wonder Father doesn't go to this kind gentleman. I've seen his name before on a circular in Father's study."

"Perhaps he has," said Dora.

But the rest of us were sure he hadn't, because, of course, if he had, there would have been more money to buy nice things. Just then Pincher jumped up and knocked over the painting-water. He is a very careless dog. I wonder why painting-water is always such an ugly colour? Dora ran for a duster to wipe it up, and H. O. dropped drops of the water on his hands and said he had got the plague. So we played at the plague for a bit, and I was an Arab physician with a bath-towel turban, and cured the plague with magic acid-drops. After that it was time for dinner, and after dinner we talked it all over and settled that we would go and see the Generous Benefactor the very next day. Of course we all wanted to go. But we thought perhaps the G. B.—it is short for Generous Benefactor—would not like it if there were so many of us. I have often noticed that it is the worst of our being six —people think six a great many, when it's children. That sentence looks wrong somehow. I mean they don't mind six pairs of boots, or six pounds of apples, or six oranges, especially in equations, but they seem to think you ought not to have five brothers and sisters. Of course Dicky was to go, because it was his idea. Dora had to go to Blackheath to see an old lady, a friend of Father's, so she couldn't go. Alice said *she* ought to go, because it said, "Ladies *and* gentlemen," and perhaps the G. B. wouldn't let us have the money unless there were both kinds of us.

H. O. said Alice wasn't a lady; and she said *he* wasn't going, anyway. Then he called her a disagreeable cat, and she began to cry.

But Oswald always tries to make up quarrels, so he said— "You're little sillies, both of you!"

And Dora said, "Don't cry, Alice; he only meant you weren't a grown-up lady."

Then H. O. said, "What else did you think I meant, Disagreeable?"

So Dicky said, "Don't be disagreeable yourself, H. O. Let her alone and say you're sorry, or I'll jolly well make you!"

So H. O. said he was sorry. Then Alice kissed him and said she was sorry too; and after that H. O. gave her a hug and said, "Now I'm *really and truly* sorry," so it was all right.

Noël went the last time any of us went to London, so he was out of it, and Dora said she would take him to Blackheath if we'd take H. O. So as there'd been a little disagreeableness we thought it was better to take him, and we did. At first we thought we'd tear our oldest things a bit more, and put some patches of different colours on them, to show the G. B. how much we wanted money. But Dora said that would be a sort of cheating, pretending we were poorer than we are. And Dora is right sometimes, though she is our elder sister. Then we thought we'd better wear our best things, so that the G. B. might see we weren't so very poor that he couldn't trust us to pay his money back when we had it. But Dora said that would be wrong too. So it came to our being quite honest, as Dora said, and going just as we were, without even washing our faces and hands; but when I looked at H. O. in the train I wished we had not been quite so particularly honest.

Every one who reads this knows what it is like to go in the train, so I shall not tell about it—though it was rather fun, especially the part where the guard came for the tickets at Waterloo, and H. O. was under the seat and pretended to be a dog without a ticket. We went to Charing Cross, and we just went round to Whitehall to see the soldiers and then by St. James's for the same reason—and when we'd looked in the shops a bit we got to Brooke Street, Bond Street. It was a brass plate on a door next to a shop—a very grand place, where they sold bonnets and hats—all very bright and smart, and no tickets on them to tell you the price. We rang a bell and a boy opened the door and we asked for Mr. Rosenbaum. The boy was not polite; he did not ask us in. So then Dicky gave him his visiting card; it was one of Father's really, but the name is the same, Mr. Richard Bastable, and we others wrote our names underneath. I happened to have a piece of pink chalk in my pocket and we wrote them with that.

Then the boy shut the door in our faces and we waited on the step. But presently he came down and asked our business. So Dicky said—

"Money advanced, young shaver; and don't be all day about it!"

And then he made us wait again, till I was quite stiff in my legs, but Alice liked it because of looking at the hats and bonnets, and at last the door opened, and the boy said—

"Mr. Rosenbaum will see you," so we wiped our feet on the mat, which said so, and we went upstairs with soft carpets and into a room. It was a beautiful room. I wished then we had put on our best things, or at least washed a little. But it was too late now.

The room had velvet curtains and a soft, soft carpet, and it was full of the most splendid things. Black and gold cabinets, and china, and statues, and pictures. There was a picture of a cabbage and a pheasant and a dead hare that was just like life, and I would have given worlds to have it for my own. The fur was so natural I should never have been tired of looking at it; but Alice liked the one of the girl with the broken jug best. Then besides the pictures there were clocks and candlesticks and vases, and gilt looking-glasses, and boxes of cigars and scent and things littered all over the chairs and tables. It was a wonderful place, and in the middle of all the splendour was a little old gentleman with a very long black coat and a very long white beard and a hooky nose—like a falcon. And he put on a pair of gold spectacles and looked at us as if he knew exactly how much our clothes were worth. And then, while we elder ones were thinking how to begin, for we had all said "Good morning" as we came in, of course, H. O. began before we could stop him. He said:

"Are you the G. B.?"

"The *what*?" said the little old gentleman.

"The G. B.," said H. O., and I winked at him to shut up, but he didn't see me, and the G. B. did. He waved his hand at *me* to shut up, so I had to, and H. O. went on—

"It stands for Generous Benefactor."

The old gentleman frowned. Then he said, "Your Father sent you here, I suppose?"

"No he didn't," said Dicky. "Why did you think so?"

The old gentleman held out the card, and I explained that we took that because Father's name happens to be the same as Dicky's.

"Doesn't he know you've come?"

"No," said Alice, "we shan't tell him till we've got the partnership, because his own business worries him a good deal and we don't want to bother him with ours till it's settled, and then we shall give him half our share."

The old gentleman took off his spectacles and rumpled his hair with his hands, then he said, "Then what *did* you come for?"

"We saw your advertisement," Dicky said, "and we want a hundred pounds on our note of hand, and my sister came so that there should be both kinds of us; and we want it to buy a partnership with in the lucrative business for sale of useful patent. No personal attendance necessary."

"I don't think I quite follow you," said the G. B. "But one thing I should like settled before entering more fully into the matter: why did you call me Generous Benefactor?"

"Well, you see," said Alice, smiling at him to show she

wasn't frightened, though I know really she was, awfully, "we thought it was so *very* kind of you to try to find out the poor people who want money and to help them and lend them your money."

"Hum!" said the G. B. "Sit down."

He cleared the clocks and vases and candlesticks off some of the chairs, and we sat down. The chairs were velvety, with gilt legs. It was like a king's palace.

"Now," he said, "you ought to be at school, instead of thinking about money. Why aren't you?"

We told him that we should go to school again when Father could manage it, but meantime we wanted to do something to restore the fallen fortunes of the House of Bastable. And we said we thought the lucrative patent would be a very good thing. He asked a lot of questions, and we told him everything we didn't think Father would mind our telling, and at last he said—

"You wish to borrow money. When will you repay it?"

"As soon as we've got it, of course," Dicky said.

Then the G. B. said to Oswald, "You seem the eldest," but I explained to him that it was Dicky's idea, so my being eldest didn't matter. Then he said to Dicky—

"You are a minor, I presume?"

Dicky said he wasn't yet, but he had thought of being a mining engineer some day, and going to Klondike.

"Minor, not miner," said the G. B. "I mean you're not of age?"

"I shall be in ten years, though," said Dicky.

"Then you might repudiate the loan," said the G. B., and Dicky said "What?" Of course he ought to have said "I beg your pardon. I didn't quite catch what you said"— that is what Oswald would have said. It is more polite than "What."

"Repudiate the loan," the G. B. repeated. "I mean you

might say you would not pay me back the money, and the law could not compel you to do so."

"Oh, well, if you think we're such sneaks," said Dicky, and he got up off his chair. But the G. B. said, "Sit down, sit down; I was only joking."

Then he talked some more, and at last he said—

"I don't advise you to enter into that partnership. It's a swindle. Many advertisements are. And I have not a hundred pounds by me to-day to lend you. But I will lend you a pound, and you can spend it as you like. And when you are twenty-one you shall pay me back."

"I shall pay you back long before that," said Dicky. "Thanks, awfully! And what about the note of hand?"

"Oh," said the G. B., "I'll trust to your honour. Between gentlemen, you know—and ladies"—he made a beautiful bow to Alice—"a word is as good as a bond."

Then he took out a sovereign, and held it in his hand while he talked to us. He gave us a lot of good advice about not going into business too young, and about doing our lessons—just swatting a bit, on our own hook, so as not to be put in a low form when we went back to school. And all the time he was stroking the sovereign and looking at it as if he thought it very beautiful. And so it was, for it was a new one. Then at last he held it out to Dicky, and when Dicky put out his hand for it the G. B. suddenly put the sovereign back in his pocket.

"No," he said, "I won't give you the sovereign. I'll give you fifteen shillings, and this nice bottle of scent. It's worth far more than the five shillings I'm charging you for it. And, when you can, you shall pay me back the pound, and sixty per cent. interest—sixty per cent., sixty per cent——"

"What's that?" said H. O.

The G. B. said he'd tell us that when we paid back the sovereign, but sixty per cent. was nothing to be afraid of.

He gave Dicky the money. And the boy was made to call a cab, and the G. B. put us in and shook hands with us all, and asked Alice to give him a kiss, so she did, and H. O. would do it too, though his face was dirtier than ever. The G. B. paid the cabman and told him what station to go to, and so we went home.

That evening Father had a letter by the seven o'clock post. And when he had read it he came up into the nursery. He did not look quite so unhappy as usual, but he looked grave.

"You've been to Mr. Rosenbaum's," he said.

So we told him all about it. It took a long time, and Father sat in the armchair. It was jolly. He doesn't often come and talk to us now. He has to spend all his time thinking about his business. And when we'd told him all about it he said—

"You haven't done any harm this time, children; rather good than harm, indeed. Mr. Rosenbaum has written me a very kind letter."

"Is he a friend of yours, Father?" Oswald asked.

"He is an acquaintance," said my father, frowning a little, "we have done some business together. And this letter——" He stopped and then said: "No; you didn't do any harm to-day; but I want you for the future not to do anything so serious as to try to buy a partnership without consulting me, that's all. I don't want to interfere with your plays and pleasures; but you will consult me about business matters won't you?"

Of course we said we should be delighted, but then Alice, who was sitting on his knee, said, "We didn't like to bother you."

Father said, "I haven't much time to be with you, for my business takes most of my time. It is an anxious business— but I can't bear to think of your being left all alone like this."

He looked so sad we all said we liked being alone. And then he looked sadder than ever.

Then Alice said, "We don't mean that exactly, Father. It *is* rather lonely sometimes, since Mother died."

Then we were all quiet a little while.

Father stayed with us till we went to bed, and when he said good night he looked quite cheerful. So we told him so, and he said—

"Well, the fact is, that letter took a weight off my mind."

I can't think what he meant—but I am sure the G. B. would be pleased if he could know he had taken a weight off anybody's mind. He is that sort of man, I think.

We gave the scent to Dora. It is not quite such good scent as we thought it would be, but we had fifteen shillings—and they were all good, so is the G. B.

And until those fifteen shillings were spent we felt almost as jolly as though our fortunes had been properly restored. You do not notice your general fortune so much, as long as you have money in your pocket. This is why so many children with regular pocket-money have never felt it their duty to seek for treasure. So, perhaps, our not having pocket-money was a blessing in disguise. But the disguise was quite impenetrable, like the villains' in the books; and it seemed still more so when the fifteen shillings were all spent. Then at last the others agreed to let Oswald try his way of seeking for treasure, but they were not at all keen about it, and many a boy less firm than Oswald would have chucked the whole thing. But Oswald knew that a hero must rely on himself alone. So he stuck to it, and presently the others saw their duty, and backed him up.

CHAPTER X

LORD TOTTENHAM

OSWALD IS a boy of firm and unswerving character, and
he had never wavered from his first idea. He felt quite certain that the books were right, and that the best way to restore fallen fortunes was to rescue an old gentleman in distress. Then he brings you up as his own son: but if you pre-
ferred to go on being your own father's son I expect the old
gentleman would make it up to you some other way. In the
books the least thing does it—you put up the railway
carriage window—or you pick up his purse when he drops
it—or you say a hymn when he suddenly asks you to, and
then your fortune is made.

The others, as I said, were very slack about it, and did not
seem to care much about trying the rescue. They said there
wasn't any deadly peril, and we should have to make one
before we could rescue the old gentleman from it, but
Oswald didn't see that that mattered. However, he thought
he would try some of the easier ways first, by himself.

So he waited about at the station, pulling up railway carriage windows for old gentlemen who looked likely—but
nothing happened, and at last the porters said he was a
nuisance. So that was no go. No one ever asked him to say a
hymn though he had learned a nice short one, beginning "New
every morning"—and when an old gentleman did drop a
two-shilling piece just by Ellis's the hairdresser's, and Oswald
picked it up, and was just thinking what he should say when
he returned it, the old gentleman caught him by the collar
and called him a young thief. It would have been very unpleasant for Oswald if he hadn't happened to be a very brave

The old gentleman caught him by the collar, and called him a young thief

boy, and knew the policeman on the beat very well indeed. So the policeman backed him up, and the old gentleman said he was sorry, and offered Oswald sixpence. Oswald refused it with polite disdain, and nothing more happened at all.

When Oswald had tried by himself and it had not come off, he said to the others, "We're wasting our time, not trying to rescue the old gentleman in deadly peril. Come—buck up! Do let's do something!"

It was dinner-time, and Pincher was going round getting the bits off the plates. There were plenty because it was cold-mutton day. And Alice said—

"It's only fair to try Oswald's way—he has tried all the things the others thought of. Why couldn't we rescue Lord Tottenham?"

Lord Tottenham is the old gentleman who walks over the Heath every day in a paper collar at three o'clock—and when he gets halfway, if there is no one about, he changes his collar and throws the dirty one into the furze-bushes.

Dicky said, "Lord Tottenham's all right—but where's the deadly peril?"

And we couldn't think of any. There are no highwaymen on Blackheath now, I am sorry to say. And though Oswald said half of us could be highwaymen and the other half rescue party, Dora kept on saying it would be wrong to be a highwayman—and so we had to give that up.

Then Alice said, "What about Pincher?"

And we all saw at once that it could be done.

Pincher is very well bred, and he does know one or two things, though we never could teach him to beg. But if you tell him to hold on—he will do it, even if you only say "Seize him!" in a whisper.

So we arranged it all. Dora said she wouldn't play; she said she thought it was wrong, and she knew it was silly—so we left her out, and she went and sat in the dining-room with a

goody book, so as to be able to say she didn't have anything
to do with it, if we got into a row over it.

Alice and H. O. were to hide in the furze-bushes just by
where Lord Tottenham changes his collar, and they were
to whisper, "Seize him!" to Pincher; and then when Pincher
had seized Lord Tottenham we were to go and rescue him
from his deadly peril. And he would say, "How can I reward you, my noble young preservers?" and it would be all
right.

So we went up to the Heath. We were afraid of being
late. Oswald told the others what Procrastination was—so
they got to the furze-bushes a little after two o'clock, and
it was rather cold. Alice and H. O. and Pincher hid, but
Pincher did not like it any more than they did, and as we
three walked up and down we heard him whining. And
Alice kept saying, "I *am* so cold! Isn't he coming yet?" And
H. O. wanted to come out and jump about to warm himself.
But we told him he must learn to be a Spartan boy, and that
he ought to be very thankful he hadn't got a beastly fox
eating his inside all the time. H. O. is our little brother, and
we are not going to let it be our fault if he grows up a milk-
sop. Besides, it was not really cold. It was his knees—he
wears socks. So they stayed where they were. And at last,
when even the other three who were walking about were
beginning to feel rather chilly, we saw Lord Tottenham's
big black cloak coming along, flapping in the wind like a
great bird. So we said to Alice—

"Hist! he approaches. You'll know when to set Pincher on
by hearing Lord Tottenham talking to himself—he always
does while he is taking off his collar."

Then we three walked slowly away whistling to show we
were not thinking of anything. Our lips were rather cold,
but we managed to do it.

Lord Tottenham came striding along, talking to himself.

People call him the mad Protectionist. I don't know what it means—but I don't think people ought to call a Lord such names.

As he passed us he said, "Ruin of the country, sir! Fatal error, fatal error!" And then we looked back and saw he was getting quite near where Pincher was, and Alice and H. O. We walked on—so that he shouldn't think we were looking—and in a minute we heard Pincher's bark, and then nothing for a bit; and then we looked round, and sure enough good old Pincher had got Lord Tottenham by the trouser leg and was holding on like billy-oh, so we started to run.

Lord Tottenham had got his collar half off—it was sticking out sideways under his ear—and he was shouting, "Help, help, murder!" exactly as if some one had explained to him beforehand what he was to do. Pincher was growling and snarling and holding on. When we got up to him I stopped and said—

"Dicky, we must rescue this good old man."

Lord Tottenham roared in his fury, "Good old man be——" something or othered. "Call the dog off!"

So Oswald said, "It is a dangerous task—but who would hesitate to do an act of true bravery?"

And all the while Pincher was worrying and snarling, and Lord Tottenham shouting to us to get the dog away. He was dancing about in the road with Pincher hanging on like grim death; and his collar flapping about, where it was undone.

Then Noël said, "Haste, ere yet it be too late." So I said to Lord Tottenham—

"Stand still, aged sir, and I will endeavour to alleviate your distress."

He stood still, and I stooped down and caught hold of Pincher and whispered, "Drop it, sir; drop it!"

Good old Pincher had got Lord Tottenham by the trouser-leg

So then Pincher dropped it, and Lord Tottenham fastened his collar again—he never does change it if there's any one looking—and he said—

"I'm much obliged, I'm sure. Nasty vicious brute! Here's something to drink my health."

But Dicky explained that we are teetotallers, and do not drink people's healths. So Lord Tottenham said, "Well, I'm much obliged any way. And now I come to look at you— of course, you're not young ruffians, but gentlemen's sons, eh? Still, you won't be above taking a tip from an old boy— I wasn't when I was your age," and he pulled out half a sovereign.

It was very silly; but now we'd done it I felt it would be beastly mean to take the old boy's chink after putting him in such a funk. He didn't say anything about bringing us up as his own sons—so I didn't know what to do. I let Pincher go, and was just going to say he was very welcome, and we'd rather not have the money, which seemed the best way out of it, when that beastly dog spoiled the whole show. Directly I let him go he began to jump about at us and bark for joy, and try to lick our faces. He was so proud of what he'd done. Lord Tottenham opened his eyes and he just said, "The dog seems to know you."

And then Oswald saw it was all up, and he said, "Good morning," and tried to get away. But Lord Tottenham said—

"Not so fast!" And he caught Noël by the collar. Noël gave a howl, and Alice ran out from the bushes. Noël is her favourite. I'm sure I don't know why. Lord Tottenham looked at her, and he said—

"So there are more of you!" And then H. O. came out.

"Do you complete the party?" Lord Tottenham asked him. And H. O. said there were only five of us this time.

Lord Tottenham turned sharp off and began to walk

away, holding Noël by the collar. We caught up with him, and asked him where he was going, and he said, "To the Police Station." So then I said quite politely, "Well, don't take Noël! he's not strong, and he easily gets upset. Besides, it wasn't his doing. If you want to take any one take me—it was my very own idea."

Dicky behaved very well. He said, "If you take Oswald I'll go too, but don't take Noël; he's such a delicate little chap."

Lord Tottenham stopped, and he said, "You should have thought of that before." Noël was howling all the time, and his face was very white, and Alice said—

"Oh, do let Noël go, dear, good, kind Lord Tottenham; he'll faint if you don't, I know he will, he does sometimes. Oh, I wish we'd never done it! Dora said it was wrong."

"Dora displayed considerable common sense," said Lord Tottenham, and he let Noël go. And Alice put her arm round Noël and tried to cheer him up, but he was all trembly, and as white as paper.

Then Lord Tottenham said—

"Will you give me your word of honour not to try to escape?"

So we said we would.

"Then follow me," he said, and led the way to a bench. We all followed, and Pincher too, with his tail between his legs—he knew something was wrong. Then Lord Tottenham sat down, and he made Oswald and Dicky and H. O. stand in front of him, but he let Alice and Noël sit down. And he said—

"You set your dog on me, and you tried to make me believe you were saving me from it. And you would have taken my half-sovereign. Such conduct is most—— No—you shall tell me what it is, sir, and speak the truth."

So I had to say it was most ungentlemanly, but I said I hadn't been going to take the half-sovereign.

"Then what did you do it for?" he asked. "The truth, mind."

So I said, "I see now it was very silly, and Dora said it was wrong, but it didn't seem so till we did it. We wanted to restore the fallen fortunes of our house, and in the books if you rescue an old gentleman from deadly peril, he brings you up as his own son—or if you prefer to be your father's son, he starts you in business, so that you end in wealthy affluence; and there wasn't any deadly peril, so we made Pincher into one—and so——" I was so ashamed I couldn't go on, for it did seem an awfully mean thing. Lord Tottenham said—

"A very nice way to make your fortune—by deceit and trickery. I have a horror of dogs. If I'd been a weak man the shock might have killed me. What do you think of yourselves, eh?"

We were all crying except Oswald, and the others say he was; and Lord Tottenham went on—

"Well, well, I see you're sorry. Let this be a lesson to you; and we'll say no more about it. I'm an old man now, but I was young once."

Then Alice slid along the bench close to him, and put her hand on his arm: her fingers were pink through the holes in her woolly gloves, and said, "I think you're very good to forgive us, and we are really very, very sorry. But we wanted to be like the children in the books—only we never have the chances they have. Everything they do turns out all right. But we *are* sorry, very, very. And I know Oswald wasn't going to take the half-sovereign. Directly you said that about a tip from an old boy I began to feel bad inside, and I whispered to H. O. that I wished we hadn't."

Then Lord Tottenham stood up, and he looked like the

Death of Nelson, for he is clean shaved and it is a good face, and he said—

"Always remember never to do a dishonourable thing, for money or for anything else in the world."

And we promised we would remember. Then he took off his hat, and we took off ours, and he went away, and we went home. I never felt so cheap in all my life! Dora said, "I told you so," but we didn't mind even that so much, though it was indeed hard to bear. It was what Lord Tottenham had said about ungentlemanly. We didn't go on to the Heath for a week after that; but at last we all went, and we waited for him by the bench. When he came along Alice said, "Please, Lord Tottenham, we have not been on the Heath for a week, to be a punishment because you let us off. And we have brought you a present each if you will take them to show you are willing to make it up."

He sat down on the bench, and we gave him our presents. Oswald gave him a sixpenny compass—he bought it with my own money on purpose to give him. Oswald always buys useful presents. The needle would not move after I'd had it a day or two, but Lord Tottenham used to be an admiral, so he will be able to make that go all right. Alice had made him a shaving-case, with a rose worked on it. And H. O. gave him his knife—the same one he once cut all the buttons off his best suit with. Dicky gave him his prize, *Naval Heroes*, because it was the best thing he had, and Noël gave him a piece of poetry he had made himself:

> When sin and shame bow down the brow
> Then people feel just like we do now.
> We are so sorry with grief and pain
> We never will be so ungentlemanly again.

Lord Tottenham seemed very pleased. He thanked us, and talked to us for a bit, and when he said good-bye he said—

"All's fair weather now, mates," and shook hands.

And whenever we meet him he nods to us, and if the girls are with us he takes off his hat, so he can't really be going on thinking us ungentlemanly now.

CHAPTER XI

CASTILIAN AMOROSO

ONE DAY when we suddenly found that we had half a crown we decided that we really ought to try Dicky's way of restoring our fallen fortunes while yet the deed was in our power. Because it might easily have happened to us never to have half a crown again. So we decided to dally no longer with being journalists and bandits and things like them, but to send for sample and instructions how to earn two pounds a week each in our spare time. We had seen the advertisement in the paper, and we had always wanted to do it, but we had never had the money to spare before, somehow. The advertisement says: "Any lady or gentleman can easily earn two pounds a week in their spare time. Sample and instructions, two shillings. Packed free from observation." A good deal of the half-crown was Dora's. It came from her godmother; but she said she would not mind letting Dicky have it if he would pay her back before Christmas, and if we were sure it was right to try to make our fortune that way. Of course that was quite easy because out of two pounds a week in your spare time you can easily pay all your debts, and have almost as much left as you began with; and as to right we told her to dry up.

Dicky had always thought that this was really the best way to restore our fallen fortunes, and we were glad that now he had a chance of trying, because of course we wanted the two pounds a week each, and besides, we were rather tired of Dicky's always saying, when our ways didn't turn out well, "Why don't you try the sample and instructions about our spare time?"

When we found out about our half-crown we got the paper. Noël was playing admirals in it, but he had made the cocked hat without tearing the paper, and we found the advertisement, and it said just the same as ever. So we got a two-shilling postal order and a stamp, and what was left of the money it was agreed we would spend in ginger-beer to drink success to trade.

We got some nice paper out of Father's study, and Dicky wrote the letter, and we put in the money and put on the stamp, and made H. O. post it. Then we drank the ginger-beer, and then we waited for the sample and instructions. It seemed a long time coming, and the postman got quite tired of us running out and stopping him in the street to ask if it had come.

But on the third morning it came. It was quite a large parcel, and it was packed, as the advertisement said it would be, "free from observation." That means it was in a box; and inside the box was some stiff browny cardboard, crinkled like the galvanized iron on the tops of chicken-houses, and inside that was a lot of paper, some of it printed and some scrappy, and in the very middle of it all a bottle, not very large, and black, and sealed on the top of the cork with yellow sealing-wax.

We looked at it as it lay on the nursery table, and while all the others grabbed at the papers to see what the printing said, Oswald went to look for the corkscrew, so as to see what was inside the bottle. He found the corkscrew in the dresser drawer—it always gets there, though it is supposed to be in the sideboard drawer in the dining-room—and when he got back the others had read most of the printed papers.

"I don't think it's much good, and I don't think it's quite nice to sell wine," Dora said; "and besides, it's not easy to suddenly begin to sell things when you aren't used to it."

"I don't know," said Alice; "I believe I could."

They all looked rather down in the mouth, though, and Oswald asked how you were to make your two pounds a week.

"Why, you've got to get people to taste that stuff in the bottle. It's sherry—Castilian Amoroso its name is—and then you get them to buy it, and then you write to the people and tell them the other people want the wine, and then for every dozen you sell you get two shillings from the wine people, so if you sell twenty dozen a week you get your two pounds. I don't think we shall sell as much as that," said Dicky.

"We might not for the first week," Alice said, "but when people found out how nice it was, they would want more and more. And if we only got ten shillings a week it would be something to begin with, wouldn't it?"

Oswald said he should jolly well think it would, and then Dicky took the cork out with the corkscrew. The cork broke a good deal, and some of the bits went into the bottle. Dora got the medicine glass that has the teaspoons and table-spoons marked on it, and we agreed to have a teaspoonful each, to see what it was like.

"No one must have more than that," Dora said, "however nice it is." Dora behaved rather as if it were her bottle. I suppose it was, because she had lent the money for it.

Then she measured out the teaspoonful, and she had first go, because of being the eldest. We asked at once what it was like, but Dora could not speak just then.

Then she said, "It's like the tonic Noël had in the spring; but perhaps sherry ought to be like that."

Then it was Oswald's turn. He thought it was very burny; but he said nothing. He wanted to see first what the others would say.

Dicky said his was simply beastly, and Alice said Noël could taste next if he liked.

Noël said it was the golden wine of the gods, but he had to put his handkerchief up to his mouth all the same, and I saw the face he made.

Then H. O. had his, and he spat it out in the fire, which was very rude and nasty, and we told him so.

Then it was Alice's turn. She said, "Only half a teaspoonful for me, Dora. We mustn't use it all up." And she tasted it and said nothing.

Then Dicky said: "Look here, I chuck this. I'm not going to hawk round such beastly stuff. Any one who likes can have the bottle. *Quis?*"

And Alice got out "*Ego*" before the rest of us. Then she said, "I know what's the matter with it. It wants sugar."

And at once we all saw that that was all there was the matter with the stuff. So we got two lumps of sugar and crushed it on the floor with one of the big wooden bricks till it was powdery, and mixed it with some of the wine up to the tablespoon mark, and it was quite different, and not nearly so nasty.

"You see it's all right when you get used to it," Dicky said. I think he was sorry he had said "*Quis?*" in such a hurry.

"Of course," Alice said, "it's rather dusty. We must crush the sugar carefully in clean paper before we put it in the bottle."

Dora said she was afraid it would be cheating to make our bottle nicer than what people would get when they ordered a dozen bottles, but Alice said Dora always made a fuss about everything, and really it would be quite honest.

"You see," she said, "I shall just tell them, quite truthfully, what we have done to it, and when their dozens come they can do it for themselves."

So then we crushed eight more lumps, very cleanly and carefully between newspapers, and shook it up well in the bottle, and corked it up with a screw of paper, brown and not news, for fear of the poisonous printing ink getting wet and dripping down into the wine and killing people. We made Pincher have a taste, and he sneezed for ever so long, and after that he used to go under the sofa whenever we showed him the bottle.

Then we asked Alice who she would try and sell it to. She said: "I shall ask everybody who comes to the house. And while we are doing that, we can be thinking of outside people to take it to. We must be careful: there's not much more than half of it left, even counting the sugar."

We did not wish to tell Eliza—I don't know why. And she opened the door very quickly that day, so that the Taxes and a man who came to our house by mistake for next door got away before Alice had a chance to try them with the Castilian Amoroso. But about five Eliza slipped out for half an hour to see a friend who was making her a hat for Sunday, and while she was gone there was a knock.

Alice went, and we looked over the banisters.

When she opened the door, she said at once, "Will you walk in, please?"

The person at the door said, "I called to see your Pa, miss. Is he at home?"

Alice said again, "Will you walk in, please?"

Then the person—it sounded like a man—said, "He *is* in, then?" But Alice only kept on saying, "Will you walk in, please?" So at last the man did, rubbing his boots very loudly on the mat. Then Alice shut the front door, and we saw that it was the butcher, with an envelope in his hand. He was not dressed in blue, like when he is cutting up the sheep and things in the shop, and he wore knickerbockers. Alice says he came on a bicycle. She led the way into the dining-room, where the Castilian Amoroso bottle and the medicine glass were standing on the table all ready.

The others stayed on the stairs, but Oswald crept down and looked through the door-rack.

"Please sit down," said Alice quite calmly, though she told me afterwards I had no idea how silly she felt. And the butcher sat down. Then Alice stood quite still and said nothing, but she fiddled with the medicine glass and put the screw of brown paper straight in the Castilian bottle.

"Will you tell your Pa I'd like a word with him?" the butcher said, when he got tired of saying nothing.

"He'll be in very soon, I think," Alice said.

And then she stood still again and said nothing. It was beginning to look very idiotic of her, and H. O. laughed. I went back and cuffed him for it quite quietly, and I don't think the butcher heard. But Alice did, and it roused her from her stupor. She spoke suddenly, very fast indeed—so fast that I knew she had made up what she was going to say before. She had got most of it out of the circular.

She said, "I want to call your attention to a sample of sherry wine I have here. It is called Castilian something or other, and at the price it is unequalled for flavour and bouquet."

The butcher said, "Well—I never!"

And Alice went on, "Would you like to taste it?"

"Thank you very much, I'm sure, miss," said the butcher. Alice poured some out.

The butcher tasted a very little. He licked his lips and we thought he was going to say how good it was. But he did not. He put down the medicine glass with nearly all the stuff left in it (we put it back in the bottle afterwards to save waste) and said, "Excuse me, miss, but isn't it a little sweet? —for sherry I mean?"

"The *real* isn't," said Alice. "If you order a dozen it will come quite different to that—we like it best with sugar. I wish you *would* order some."

The butcher asked why.

Alice did not speak for a minute, and then she said—

"I don't mind telling *you*: you are in business yourself, aren't you? We are trying to get people to buy it, because we shall have two shillings for every dozen we can make any one buy. It's called a purr something."

"A percentage. Yes, I see," said the butcher, looking at the hole in the carpet.

"You see there are reasons," Alice went on, "why we want to make our fortunes as quickly as we can."

"Quite so," said the butcher, and he looked at the place where the paper is coming off the wall.

"And this seems a good way," Alice went on. "We paid two shillings for the sample and instructions, and it says you can make two pounds a week easily in your leisure time."

"I'm sure I hope you may, miss," said the butcher.

And Alice said again would he buy some?

"Sherry is my favourite wine," he said.

Alice asked him to have some more to drink.

"No, thank you, miss," he said; "it's my favourite wine, but it doesn't agree with me; not the least bit. But I've an uncle drinks it. Suppose I ordered him half a dozen for a Christmas present? Well, miss, here's the shilling commission, anyway," and he pulled out a handful of money and gave her the shilling.

"But I thought the wine people paid that," Alice said.

But the butcher said not on half-dozens they didn't. Then he said he didn't think he'd wait any longer for Father—but would Alice ask Father to write him?

Alice offered him the sherry again, but he said something

about "Not for worlds!"—and then she let him out and came back to us with the shilling, and said, "How's that?" And we said "A 1."

And all the evening we talked of our fortune that we had begun to make.

Nobody came next day, but the day after a lady came to ask for money to build an orphanage for the children of dead sailors. And we saw her. I went in with Alice. And when we had explained to her that we had only a shilling and we wanted it for something else, Alice suddenly said, "Would you like some wine?"

And the lady said, "Thank you very much," but she looked surprised. She was not a young lady, and she had a mantle with beads, and the beads had come off in places— leaving a browny braid showing, and she had printed papers about the dead sailors in a sealskin bag, and the seal had come off in places, leaving the skin bare.

We gave her a tablespoonful of the wine in a proper wine-glass out of the sideboard, because she was a lady. And when she had tasted it she got up in a very great hurry, and shook out her dress and snapped her bag shut, and said, "You naughty, wicked children! What do you mean by playing a trick like this? You ought to be ashamed of yourselves! I shall write to your Mamma about it. You dreadful little girl! —you might have poisoned me. But your Mamma. . . ."

Then Alice said, "I'm very sorry; the butcher liked it, only he said it was sweet. And please don't write to Mother. It makes Father so unhappy when letters come for her"— and Alice was very near crying.

"What do you mean, you silly child?" said the lady, looking quite bright and interested. "Why doesn't your Father like your Mother to have letters—eh?"

And Alice said, "*Oh*, you . . . !" and began to cry, and bolted out of the room.

Then I said, "Our Mother is dead, and will you please go away now?"

The lady looked at me a minute, and then she looked quite different, and she said, "I'm very sorry. I didn't know. Never mind about the wine. I daresay your little sister meant it kindly." And she looked round the room just like the butcher had done. Then she said again, "I didn't know—I'm very sorry. . . ."

So I said, "Don't mention it," and shook hands with her, and let her out. Of course we couldn't have asked her to buy the wine after what she'd said. But I think she was not a bad sort of person. I do like a person to say they're sorry when they ought to be—especially a grown-up. They do it so seldom. I suppose that's why we think so much of it.

But Alice and I didn't feel jolly for ever so long afterwards. And when I went back into the dining-room I saw how different it was from when Mother was here, and we are different, and Father is different, and nothing is like it was. I am glad I am not made to think about it every day.

I went and found Alice, and told her what the lady had said, and when she had finished crying we put away the bottle and said we would not try to sell any more to people who came. And we did not tell the others—we only said the lady did not buy any—but we went up on the Heath, and some soldiers went by and there was a Punch-and-Judy show, and when we came back we were better.

The bottle got quite dusty where we had put it, and perhaps the dust of ages would have laid thick and heavy on it, only a clergyman called when we were all out. He was not our own clergyman—Mr. Bristow is our own clergyman, and we all love him, and we would not try to sell sherry to people we like, and make two pounds a week out of them in our spare time. It was another clergyman, just a stray one; and he asked Eliza if the dear children would not like to come to his little Sunday school. We always spend Sunday afternoons with Father. But as he had left the name of his vicarage with Eliza, and asked her to tell us to come, we thought we would go and call on him, just to explain about Sunday afternoons, and we thought we might as well take the sherry with us.

"I won't go unless you all go too," Alice said, "and I won't do the talking."

Dora said she thought we had much better not go; but we said "Rot!" and it ended in her coming with us, and I am glad she did.

Oswald said he would do the talking if the others liked, and he learned up what to say from the printed papers.

We went to the Vicarage early on Saturday afternoon, and rang at the bell. It is a new red house with no trees in the garden, only very yellow mould and gravel. It was all very neat and dry. Just before we rang the bell we heard some one inside call "Jane! Jane!" and we thought we would not be Jane for anything. It was the sound of the voice that called that made us sorry for her.

The door was opened by a very neat servant in black, with a white apron; we saw her tying the strings as she came along the hall, through the different-coloured glass in the door. Her face was red, and I think she was Jane.

We asked if we could see Mr. Mallow.

The servant said Mr. Mallow was very busy with his sermon just then, but she would see.

But Oswald said, "It's all right. He asked us to come."

So she let us all in and shut the front door, and showed us into a very tidy room with a bookcase full of a lot of books covered in black cotton with white labels, and some dull pictures and a harmonium. And Mr. Mallow was writing at a desk with drawers, copying something out of a book. He was stout and short and wore spectacles.

He covered his writing up when we went in—I didn't know why. He looked rather cross, and we heard Jane or somebody being scolded outside by the voice. I hope it wasn't for letting us in, but I have had doubts.

"Well," said the clergyman, "what is all this about?"

"You asked us to call," Dora said, "about your little Sunday school. We are the Bastables of Lewisham Road."

"Oh—ah, yes," he said; "and shall I expect you all to-morrow?" He took up his pen and fiddled with it, and he did not ask us to sit down. But some of us did.

"We always spend Sunday afternoon with Father," said Dora; "but we wished to thank you for being so kind as to ask us."

"And we wished to ask you something else!" said Oswald; and he made a sign to Alice to get the sherry ready in the glass. She did—behind Oswald's back while he was speaking.

"My time is limited," said Mr. Mallow, looking at his watch; "but still——" Then he muttered something about the fold, and went on: "Tell me what is troubling you, my little man, and I will try to give you any help in my power. What is it you want?"

Then Oswald quickly took the glass from Alice, and held it out to him, and said, "I want your opinion on that."

"On *that*," he said. "What is it?"

"It is a shipment," Oswald said; "but it's quite enough for you to taste." Alice had filled the glass half-full; I suppose she was too excited to measure properly.

"A shipment?" said the clergyman, taking the glass in his hand.

"Yes," Oswald went on; "an exceptional opportunity. Full-bodied and nutty."

"It really does taste rather like one kind of Brazil-nut." Alice put her oar in as usual.

The Vicar looked from Alice to Oswald, and back again,

and Oswald went on with what he had learned from the printing. The clergyman held the glass at half-arm's-length, stiffly, as if he had caught cold.

"It is of a quality never before offered at the price. Old Delicate Amoro—what's its name——"

"Amorolio," said H. O.

"Amoroso," said Oswald. "H. O., you just shut up—Castilian Amoroso—it's a true after-dinner wine, stimulating and yet . . ."

"*Wine?*" said Mr. Mallow, holding the glass farther off. "Do you *know*," he went on, making his voice very thick and strong (I expect he does it like that in church), "have you never been *taught* that it is the drinking of *wine* and *spirits*—yes, and BEER, which makes half the homes in England full of *wretched* little children, and *degraded*, MISERABLE parents?"

"Not if you put sugar in it," said Alice firmly; "eight lumps and shake the bottle. We have each had more than a teaspoonful of it, and we were not ill at all. It was something else that upset H. O. Most likely all those acorns he got out of the Park."

The clergyman seemed to be speechless with conflicting emotions, and just then the door opened and a lady came in. She had a white cap with lace, and an ugly violet flower in it, and she was tall, and looked very strong, though thin. And I do believe she had been listening at the door.

"But why," the Vicar was saying, "why did you bring this dreadful fluid, this curse of our country, to *me* to taste?"

"Because we thought you might buy some," said Dora, who never sees when a game is up. "In books the parson loves his bottle of old port; and new sherry is just as good—with sugar—for people who like sherry. And if you would order a dozen of the wine, then we should get two shillings."

The lady said (and it *was* the voice), "Good gracious!

Nasty, sordid little things! Haven't they any one to teach them better?"

And Dora got up and said, "No, we are not those things you say; but we are sorry we came here to be called names. We want to make our fortune just as much as Mr. Mallow does—only no one would listen to us if we preached, so it's no use our copying out sermons like him."

And I think that was smart of Dora, even if it was rather rude.

Then I said perhaps we had better go, and the lady said, "I should think so!" But when we were going to wrap up the bottle and glass the clergyman said, "No; you can leave that," and we were so upset we did, though it wasn't his after all.

We walked home very fast and not saying much, and the girls went up to their room. When I went to tell them tea was ready, and there was a teacake, Dora was crying like anything and Alice hugging her. I am afraid there is a great deal of crying in this chapter, but I can't help it. Girls will sometimes; I suppose it is their nature, and we ought to be sorry for their affliction.

"It's no good," Dora was saying, "you all hate me, and you think I'm a prig and a busybody, but I do try to do right—oh, I do! Oswald, go away; don't come here making fun of me!"

So I said, "I'm not making fun, Sissy; don't cry, old girl."

Mother taught me to call her Sissy when we were very little and before the others came, but I don't often somehow, now we are old. I patted her on the back, and she put her head against my sleeve, holding on to Alice all the time, and she went on. She was in that laughy-cryey state when people say things they wouldn't say at other times.

"Oh dear, oh dear—I do try, I do. And when Mother died she said, 'Dora, take care of the others, and teach them to be

good, and keep them out of trouble and make them happy.'
She said, 'Take care of them for me, Dora dear.' And I
have tried, and all of you hate me for it; and to-day I let
you do this, though I knew all the time it was silly."

I hope you will not think I was a muff, but I kissed Dora
for some time. Because girls like it. And I will never say again
that she comes the good elder sister too much. And I have
put all this in though I do hate telling about it, because I own
I have been hard on Dora, but I never will be again. She is
a good old sort; of course we never knew before about what
Mother told her, or we wouldn't have ragged her as we did.
We did not tell the little ones, but I got Alice to speak to
Dicky, and we three can sit on the others if requisite.

This made us forget all about the sherry; but about eight
o'clock there was a knock, and Eliza went, and we saw it was
poor Jane, if her name was Jane, from the Vicarage. She
handed in a brown-paper parcel and a letter. And three
minutes later Father called us into his study.

On the table was the brown-paper parcel, open, with our
bottle and glass on it, and Father had a letter in his hand. He
pointed to the bottle and sighed, and said, "What have you
been doing now?" The letter in his hand was covered with
little black writing, all over the four large pages.

So Dicky spoke up, and he told Father the whole thing,
as far as he knew it, for Alice and I had not told about the
dead sailors' lady.

And when he had done, Alice said, "Has Mr. Mallow
written to you to say he will buy a dozen of the sherry after
all? It is really not half bad with sugar in it."

Father said no, he didn't think clergymen could afford
such expensive wine; and he said *he* would like to taste it.
So we gave him what there was left, for we had decided
coming home that we would give up trying for the two
pounds a week in our spare time.

Father tasted it, and then he acted just as H. O. had done when he had his teaspoonful, but of course we did not say anything. Then he laughed till I thought he would never stop.

I think it was the sherry, because I am sure I have read somewhere about "wine that maketh glad the heart of man." He had only a very little, which shows that it was a good after-dinner wine, stimulating, and yet . . . I forget the rest.

But when he had done laughing he said, "It's all right, kids. Only don't do it again. The wine trade is overcrowded; and besides, I thought you promised to consult me before going into business?"

"Before buying one I thought you meant," said Dicky. "This was only on commission." And Father laughed again. I am glad we got the Castilian Amoroso, because it did really cheer Father up, and you cannot always do that, however hard you try, even if you make jokes, or give him a comic paper.

CHAPTER XII

THE NOBLENESS OF OSWALD

THE PART about his nobleness only comes at the end, but you would not understand it unless you knew how it began. It began, like nearly everything about that time, with treasure-seeking.

Of course as soon as we had promised to consult my Father about business matters we all gave up wanting to go into business. I don't know how it is, but having to consult about a thing with grown-up people, even the bravest and the best, seems to make the thing not worth doing afterwards.

We don't mind Albert's uncle chipping in sometimes when the thing's going on, but we are glad he never asked us to promise to consult him about anything. Yet Oswald saw that my Father was quite right; and I daresay if we had had that hundred pounds we should have spent it on the share in that lucrative business for the sale of useful patent, and then found out afterwards that we should have done better to spend the money in some other way. My Father says so, and he ought to know. We had several ideas about that time, but having so little chink always stood in the way. This was the case with H. O.'s idea of setting up a coconut-shy on this side of the Heath, where there are none generally. We had no sticks or wooden balls, and the greengrocer said he could not book so many as twelve dozen coconuts without Mr. Bastable's written order. And as we did not wish to consult my Father it was decided to drop it. And when Alice dressed up Pincher in some of the dolls' clothes and we made up our minds to take him round with an organ as soon as we had taught him to dance, we were stopped at once by Dicky's remembering how he had once heard that an organ cost seven hundred pounds. Of course this was the big church kind, but even the ones on three legs can't be got for one-and-sevenpence, which was all we had when we first thought of it. So we gave that up too.

It was a wet day, I remember, and mutton hash for dinner—very tough with pale gravy with lumps in it. I think the others would have left a good deal on the sides of their plates, although they know better, only Oswald said it was a savoury stew made of the red deer that Edward shot. So then we were the Children of the New Forest, and the mutton tasted much better. No one in the New Forest minds venison being tough and the gravy pale.

Then after dinner we let the girls have a dolls' tea-party, on condition they didn't expect us boys to wash up; and it was when we were drinking the last of the liquorice water out of the little cups that Dicky said—

"This reminds me."

So we said, "What of?"

Dicky answered us at once, though his mouth was full of bread with liquorice stuck in it to look like cake. You should not speak with your mouth full, even to your own relations, and you shouldn't wipe your mouth on the back of your hand, but on your handkerchief, if you have one. Dicky did not do this. He said—

"Why, you remember when we first began about treasure-seeking, I said I had thought of something, only I could not tell you because I hadn't finished thinking about it."

We said "Yes."

"Well, this liquorice water——"

"Tea," said Alice softly.

"Well, tea then—made me think." He was going on to say what it made him think, but Noël interrupted and cried out. "I say; let's finish off this old tea-party and have a council of war."

So we got out the flags and the wooden sword and the drum, and Oswald beat it while the girls washed up, till Eliza came up to say she had the jumping toothache, and the noise went through her like a knife. So of course Oswald left off at once. When you are polite to Oswald he never refuses to grant your requests.

When we were all dressed up we sat down round the camp fire, and Dicky began again.

"Every one in the world wants money. Some people get it. The people who get it are the ones who see things. I have seen one thing."

Dicky stopped and smoked the pipe of peace. It is the pipe we did bubbles with in the summer, and somehow it has not got broken yet. We put tea-leaves in it for the pipe of peace, but the girls are not allowed to have any. It is not right to let girls smoke. They get to think too much of themselves if you let them do everything the same as men.

Oswald said, "Out with it."

"I see that glass bottles only cost a penny. H. O., if you dare to snigger I'll send you round selling old bottles, and you shan't have any sweets except out of the money you get for them. And the same with you, Noël."

"Noël wasn't sniggering," said Alice in a hurry; "it is only his taking so much interest in what you were saying makes him look like that. Be quiet, H. O., and don't you make faces, either. Do go on, Dicky dear."

So Dicky went on.

"There must be hundreds of millions of bottles of medicines sold each year. Because all the different medicines say, 'Thousands of cures daily,' and if you only take that as two thousand, which it must be, at least, it mounts up. And the people who sell them must make a great deal of money by them because they are nearly always two-and-ninepence the bottle, and three-and-six for one nearly double the size. Now the bottles, as I was saying, don't cost anything like that."

"It's the medicines costs the money," said Dora; "look how expensive jujubes are at the chemist's, and peppermints too."

"That's only because they're nice," Dicky explained; "nasty things are not so dear. Look what a lot of brimstone you get for a penny, and the same with alum. We would not put the nice kinds of chemist's things in our medicine."

Then he went on to tell us that when we had invented our medicine we would write and tell the editor about it, and he would put it in the paper, and then people would send their two-and-ninepence and three-and-six for the bottle nearly double the size, and then when the medicine had cured them they would write to the paper and their letters would be printed, saying how they had been suffering for years, and never thought to get about again, but thanks to the blessing of our ointment——

Dora interrupted and said, "Not ointment—it's so messy." And Alice thought so too. And Dicky said he did not mean it, he was quite decided to let it be in bottles. So now it was all settled, and we did not see at the time that this would be a sort of going into business, but afterwards when Albert's uncle showed us we saw it, and we were sorry. We only had to invent the medicine. You might think that was easy, because of the number of them you see every day in the paper, but it is much harder than you think. First we had to decide what sort of illness we should like to cure, and a "heated discussion ensued," like in Parliament.

Dora wanted it to be something to make the complexion of dazzling fairness, but we remembered how her face came all red and rough when she used the Rosabella soap, that was advertised to make the darkest complexion fair as the lily, and she agreed that perhaps it was better not. Noël wanted to make the medicine first and then find out what it would cure, but Dicky thought not, because there are so many more medicines than there are things the matter with us, so it would be easier to choose the disease first.

Oswald would have liked wounds. I still think it was a good idea, but Dicky said, "Who has wounds, especially now there aren't any wars? We shouldn't sell a bottle a day!" So Oswald gave in because he knows what manners are, and it was Dicky's idea. H. O. wanted a cure for the uncomfortable feeling that they give you powders for, but we explained to him that grown-up people do not have this feeling, however much they eat, and he agreed. Dicky said he did not care a straw what the loathsome disease was, as long as we hurried up and settled on something. Then Alice said—

"It ought to be something very common, and only one thing. Not the pains in the back and all the hundreds of things the people have in somebody's syrup. What's the commonest thing of all?"

And at once we said, "Colds."

So that was settled.

Then we wrote a label to go on the bottle. When it was written it would not go on the vinegar bottle that we had got, but we knew it would go small when it was printed. It was like this:

BASTABLE'S

CERTAIN CURE FOR COLDS

Coughs, Asthma, Shortness of Breath, and all infections of the Chest

One dose gives immediate relief.
It will cure your cold in one bottle
Especially the larger size at 3s. 6d.
Order at once of the Makers
To prevent disappointment

Makers:
D., O., R., A., N., & H. O. Bastable,
150, Lewisham Road, S.E.
(*A halfpenny for all bottles returned*)

Of course the next thing was for one of us to catch a cold and try what cured it; we all wanted to be the one, but it was Dicky's idea, and he said he was not going to be done out of it, so we let him. It was only fair. He left off his undershirt that very day, and next morning he stood in a draught in his nightgown for quite a long time. And we damped his day-shirt with the nail-brush before he put it on. But all was vain. They always tell you that these things will give you cold, but we found it was not so.

So then we all went over to the Park, and Dicky went right into the water with his boots on, and stood there as long as he could bear it, for it was rather cold, and we stood and cheered him on. He walked home in his wet clothes, which they say is a sure thing, but it was no go, though his boots were quite spoiled. And three days after Noël began to cough and sneeze.

So then Dicky said it was not fair.

"I can't help it," Noël said. "You should have caught it yourself, then it wouldn't have come to me."

And Alice said she had known all along Noël oughtn't to have stood about on the bank cheering in the cold.

Noël had to go to bed, and then we began to make the medicines; we were sorry he was out of it, but he had the fun of taking the things.

We made a great many medicines. Alice made herb tea. She got sage and thyme and savory and marjoram and boiled them all up together with salt and water, but she would put parsley in too. Oswald is sure parsley is not a herb. It is only put on the cold meat and you are not supposed to eat it. It kills parrots to eat parsley, I believe. I expect it was the parsley that disagreed so with Noël. The medicine did not seem to do the cough any good.

Oswald got a pennyworth of alum, because it is so cheap, and some turpentine which every one knows is good for colds, and a little sugar and an aniseed ball. These were mixed in a bottle with water, but Eliza threw it away and said it was nasty rubbish, and I hadn't any money to get more things with.

Dora made him some gruel, and he said it did his chest good; but of course that was no use, because you cannot put gruel in bottles and say it is medicine. It would not be honest, and besides nobody would believe you.

Dick mixed up lemon-juice and sugar and a little of the juice of the red flannel that Noël's throat was done up in. It comes out beautifully in hot water. Noël took this and he liked it. Noël's own idea was liquorice-water, and we let him have it, but it is too plain and black to sell in bottles at the proper price.

Noël liked H. O.'s medicine the best, which was silly of him, because it was only peppermints melted in hot water, and a little cobalt to make it look blue. It was all right, because H. O.'s paint-box is the French kind, with *Couleurs non Vénéneuses* on it. This means you may suck your brushes if you want to, or even your paints if you are a very little boy.

It was rather jolly while Noël had that cold. He had a fire in his bedroom which opens out of Dicky's and Oswald's, and the girls used to read aloud to Noël all day; they will not read aloud to you when you are well. Father was away at Liverpool on business, and Albert's uncle was at Hastings. We were rather glad of this, because we wished to give all the medicines a fair trial, and grown-ups are but too fond of interfering. As if we should have given him anything poisonous!

His cold went on—it was bad in his head, but it was not one of the kind when he has to have poultices and can't sit up in bed. But when it had been in his head nearly a week, Oswald happened to tumble over Alice on the stairs. When we got up she was crying.

"Don't cry, silly!" said Oswald; "you know I didn't hurt you." I was very sorry if I had hurt her, but you ought not to sit on the stairs in the dark and let other people tumble over you. You ought to remember how beastly it is for them if they do hurt you.

"Oh, it's not that, Oswald," Alice said. "Don't be a pig! I am so miserable. Do be kind to me."

So Oswald thumped her on the back and told her to shut up.

"It's about Noël," she said. "I'm sure he's very ill; and playing about with medicines is all very well, but I know he's ill, and Eliza won't send for the doctor: she says it's only a cold. And I know the doctor's bills are awful. I heard Father telling Aunt Emily so in the summer. But he *is* ill, and perhaps he'll die or something."

Then she began to cry again. Oswald thumped her again, because he knows how a good brother ought to behave, and said, "Cheer up." If we had been in a book Oswald would have embraced his little sister tenderly, and mingled his tears with hers.

Then Oswald said, "Why not write to Father?" And she cried more and said, "I've lost the paper with the address. H. O. had it to draw on the back of, and I can't find it now; I've looked everywhere. I'll tell you what I'm going to do. No I won't. But I'm going out. Don't tell the others. And I say, Oswald, do pretend I'm in if Eliza asks. Promise."

"Tell me what you're going to do," I said. But she said

"No"; and there was a good reason why not. So I said I wouldn't promise if it came to that. Of course I meant to all right. But it did seem mean of her not to tell me.

So Alice went out by the side door while Eliza was setting tea, and she was a long time gone; she was not in to tea. When Eliza asked Oswald where she was he said he did not know, but perhaps she was tidying her corner drawer. Girls often do this, and it takes a long time. Noël coughed a good bit after tea, and asked for Alice. Oswald told him she was doing something and it was a secret. Oswald did not tell any lies even to save his sister. When Alice came back she was very quiet, but she whispered to Oswald that it was all right. When it was rather late Eliza said she was going out to post a letter. This always takes her an hour, because she will go to the post-office across the Heath instead of the pillar-box, because once a boy dropped fusees in our pillar-box and burnt the letters. It was not any of us; Eliza told us about it. And when there was a knock at the door a long time after we thought it was Eliza come back, and that she had forgotten the back-door key. We made H. O. go down to open the door, because it is his place to run about: his legs are younger than ours. And we heard boots on the stairs besides H. O.'s, and we listened spell-bound till the door opened, and it was Albert's uncle. He looked very tired.

"I am glad you've come," Oswald said. "Alice began to think Noël——"

Alice stopped me, and her face was very red, her nose was shiny too, with having cried so much before tea.

She said, "I only said I thought Noël ought to have the doctor. Don't you think he ought?" She got hold of Albert's uncle and held on to him.

"Let's have a look at you, young man," said Albert's uncle, and he sat down on the edge of the bed. It is a rather shaky bed, the bar that keeps it steady underneath got broken when we were playing burglars last winter. It was our crowbar. He began to feel Noël's pulse, and went on talking.

"It was revealed to the great Arab physician as he made merry in his tents on the wild plains of Hastings that the Presence had a cold in its head. So he immediately seated himself on the magic carpet, and bade it bear him hither, only pausing in the flight to purchase a few sweetmeats in the bazaar."

He pulled out a jolly lot of chocolate and some butterscotch, and grapes for Noël. When we had all said thank you, he went on.

"The physician's are the words of wisdom: it's high time this kid was asleep. I have spoken. Ye have my leave to depart."

So we bunked, and Dora and Albert's uncle made Noël comfortable for the night.

Then they came to the nursery which we had gone down to, and he sat down in the Guy Fawkes' chair and said, "Now then."

Alice said, "You may tell them what I did. I daresay they'll all be in a wax, but I don't care."

"I think you were very wise," said Albert's uncle, pulling her close to him to sit on his knee. "I am very glad you telegraphed."

So then Oswald understood what Alice's secret was. She had gone out and sent a telegram to Albert's uncle at Hastings. But Oswald thought she might have told him. Afterwards she told me what she had put in the telegram. It was, "Come home. We have given Noël a cold, and I think we are killing him." With the address it came to tenpence-halfpenny.

Then Albert's uncle began to ask questions, and it all came out, how Dicky had tried to catch the cold, but the cold had gone to Noël instead, and about the medicines and all. Albert's uncle looked very serious.

"Look here," he said, "you're old enough not to play the fool like this. Health is the best thing you've got; you ought to know better than to risk it. You might have killed your little brother with your precious medicines. You've had a lucky escape, certainly. But poor Noël!"

"Oh, do you think he's going to die?" Alice asked that, and she was crying again.

"No, no," said Albert's uncle; "but look here. Do you see how silly you've been? And I thought you promised your Father——" And then he gave us a long talking-to. He can make you feel most awfully small. At last he stopped, and we said we were very sorry, and he said, "You know I promised to take you all to the pantomime?"

So we said, "Yes," and knew but too well that now he wasn't going to. Then he went on—

"Well, I will take you if you like, or I will take Noël to the sea for a week to cure his cold. Which is it to be?"

Of course he knew we should say, "Take Noël," and we did; but Dicky told me afterwards he thought it was hard on H. O.

Albert's uncle stayed till Eliza came in, and then he said good night in a way that showed us that all was forgiven and forgotten.

And we went to bed. It must have been the middle of the night when Oswald woke up suddenly, and there was Alice with her teeth chattering, shaking him to wake him.

"Oh, Oswald!" she said, "I am so unhappy. Suppose I should die in the night!"

Oswald told her to go to bed and not gas. But she said, "I must tell you; I wish I'd told Albert's uncle. I'm a thief, and if I die to-night I know where thieves go to."

So Oswald saw it was no good and he sat up in bed and said—

"Go ahead."

So Alice stood shivering and said—

"I hadn't enough money for the telegram, so I took the bad sixpence out of the exchequer. And I paid for it with that and the fivepence I had. And I wouldn't tell you because if you'd stopped me doing it I couldn't have borne it; and if you'd helped me you'd have been a thief too. Oh, what shall I do?"

Oswald thought a minute, and then said—

"You'd better have told me. But I think it will be all right if we pay it back. Go to bed. Cross with you? No, stupid! Only another time you'd better not keep secrets." So she kissed Oswald, and he let her, and she went back to bed. The next day Albert's uncle took Noël away, before Oswald had time to persuade Alice that we ought to tell him about the sixpence. Alice was very unhappy, but not so much as in the night: you can be very miserable in the night if you have done anything wrong and you happen to be awake. I know this for a fact.

None of us had any money except Eliza, and she wouldn't give us any unless we said what for; and of course we could not do that because of the honour of the family. And Oswald was anxious to get the sixpence to give to the telegraph people because he feared that the badness of that sixpence might have been found out, and that the police might come for Alice at any moment. I don't think I ever had such an unhappy day. Of course we could have written to Albert's uncle, but it would have taken a long time, and every moment of delay added to Alice's danger. We thought and thought, but we couldn't think of any way to get that sixpence. It seems a small sum, but you see Alice's liberty depended on it. It was quite late in the afternoon when I met

Mrs. Leslie on the Parade. She had a brown fur coat and a lot of yellow flowers in her hands. She stopped to speak to me, and asked me how the Poet was. I told her he had a cold, and I wondered whether she would lend me sixpence if I asked her, but I could not make up my mind how to begin to say it. It is a hard thing to say—much harder than you would think. She talked to me for a bit, and then she suddenly got into a cab and said—

"I'd no idea it was so late," and told the man where to go. And just as she started she shoved the yellow flowers through the window and said, "For the sick poet, with my love," and was driven off.

Gentle reader, I will not conceal from you what Oswald did. He knew all about not disgracing the family, and he did not like doing what I am going to say: and they were really Noël's flowers, only he could not have sent them to Hastings, and Oswald knew he would say "Yes" if Oswald asked him. Oswald sacrificed his family pride because of his little sister's danger. I do not say he was a noble boy—I just tell you what he did, and you can decide for yourself about the nobleness.

He put on his oldest clothes—they're much older than any you would think he had if you saw him when he was tidy— and he took those yellow chrysanthemums and he walked with them to Greenwich Station and waited for the trains bringing people from London. He sold those flowers in penny bunches and got tenpence. Then he went to the telegraph office at Lewisham, and said to the lady there:

"A little girl gave you a bad sixpence yesterday. Here are six good pennies."

The lady said she had not noticed it, and never mind, but Oswald knew that "Honesty is the best Policy," and he refused to take back the pennies. So at last she said she should put them in the plate on Sunday. She is a very nice lady. I like the way she does her hair.

Then Oswald went home to Alice and told her, and she hugged him, and said he was a dear, good, kind boy, and he said "Oh, it's all right."

We bought peppermint bullseyes with the fourpence I had over, and the others wanted to know where we got the money, but we would not tell.

Only afterwards when Noël came home we told him, because they were his flowers, and he said it was quite right. He made some poetry about it. I only remember one bit of it.

> The noble youth of high degree
>   Consents to play a menial part,
> All for his sister Alice's sake,
>   Who was so dear to his faithful heart.

But Oswald himself has never bragged about it.

We got no treasure out of this, unless you count the peppermint bullseyes.

CHAPTER XIII

THE ROBBER AND THE BURGLAR

A DAY OR two after Noël came back from Hastings there was snow: it was jolly. And we cleared it off the path. A man to do it is sixpence at least, and you should always save when you can. A penny saved is a penny earned. And then we thought it would be nice to clear it off the top of the portico, where it lies so thick, and the edges as if they had been cut with a knife. And just as we had got out of the landing-window on to the portico, the Water Rates came up the path with his book that he tears the thing out of that says how much you have got to pay, and the little ink-bottle hung on to his buttonhole in case you should pay him. Father says the Water Rates is a sensible man, and knows it is always well to be prepared for whatever happens, however unlikely. Alice said afterwards that she rather liked the Water Rates, really, and Noël said he had a face like a good vizier, or the man who rewards the honest boy for restoring the purse, but we did not think about these things at the time, and as the Water Rates came up the steps, we shovelled down a great square slab of snow like an avalanche —and it fell right on his head. Two of us thought of it at the same moment, so it was quite a large avalanche. And when the Water Rates had shaken himself he rang the bell. It was Saturday, and Father was at home. We know now that it is very wrong and ungentlemanly to shovel snow off porticoes on to the Water Rates, or any other person, and we hope he did not catch a cold, and we are very sorry. We apologized to the Water Rates when Father told us to. We were all sent to bed for it.

We all deserved the punishment, because the others would

have shovelled down snow just as we did if they'd thought of it—only they are not so quick at thinking of things as we are. And even quite wrong things sometimes lead to adventures; as every one knows who has ever read about pirates or highwaymen.

Eliza hates us to be sent to bed early, because it means her having to bring meals up, and it means lighting the fire in Noël's room ever so much earlier than usual. He had to have a fire because he still had a bit of a cold. But this particular day we got Eliza into a good temper by giving her a horrid brooch with pretending amethysts in it, that an aunt once gave to Alice, so Eliza brought up an extra scuttle of coals; and when the greengrocer came with the potatoes (he is always late on Saturdays) she got some chestnuts from him. So that when we heard Father go out after his dinner, there was a jolly fire in Noël's room, and we were able to go in and be Red Indians in blankets most comfortably. Eliza had gone out; she says she gets things cheaper on Saturday nights. She has a great friend, who sells fish at a shop, and he is very generous, and lets her have herrings for less than half the natural price.

So we were all alone in the house; Pincher was out with Eliza, and we talked about robbers. And Dora thought it would be a dreadful trade, but Dicky said—

"I think it would be very interesting. And you would only rob rich people, and be very generous to the poor and needy, like Claude Duval."

Dora said, "It is wrong to be a robber."

"Yes," said Alice, "you would never know a happy hour. Think of trying to sleep with the stolen jewels under your bed, and remembering all the quantities of policemen and detectives that there are in the world!"

"There are ways of being robbers that are not wrong," said Noël; "if you can rob a robber it is a right act."

"But you can't," said Dora; "he is too clever, and besides, it's wrong anyway."

"Yes you can, and it isn't; and murdering him with boiling oil is a right act too, so there!" said Noël. "What about Ali Baba? Now then!" And we felt it was a score for Noël.

"What would you do if there *was* a robber?" said Alice.

H. O. said he would kill him with boiling oil; but Alice explained that she meant a real robber—now—this minute—in the house.

Oswald and Dicky did not say; but Noël said he thought it would only be fair to ask the robber quite politely and quietly to go away, and then if he didn't you could deal with him.

Now what I am going to tell you is a very strange and wonderful thing, and I hope you will be able to believe it. I should not, if a boy told me, unless I knew him to be a man of honour, and perhaps not then unless he gave his sacred word. But it is true, all the same, and it only shows that the days of romance and daring deeds are not yet at an end.

Alice was just asking Noël *how* he would deal with the robber who wouldn't go if he was asked politely and quietly, when we heard a noise downstairs—quite a plain noise, not the kind of noise you fancy you hear. It was like somebody moving a chair. We held our breath and listened—and then came another noise, like some one poking a fire. Now, you remember there was no one *to* poke a fire or move a chair downstairs, because Eliza and Father were both out. They could not have come in without our hearing them, because the front door is as hard to shut as the back one, and which-ever you go in by you have to give a slam that you can hear all down the street.

H. O. and Alice and Dora caught hold of each other's

blankets and looked at Dicky and Oswald, and every one was quite pale. And Noël whispered—

"It's ghosts, I know it is"—and then we listened again, but there was no more noise. Presently Dora said in a whisper—

"Whatever shall we do? Oh, whatever shall we do—what *shall* we do?"

And she kept on saying it till we had to tell her to shut up.

O reader, have you ever been playing Red Indians in blankets round a bedroom fire in a house where you thought there was no one but you—and then suddenly heard a noise like a chair, and a fire being poked, downstairs? Unless you have you will not be able to imagine at all what it feels like. It was not like in books; our hair did not stand on end at all, and we never said "Hist!" once, but our feet got very cold, though we were in blankets by the fire, and the insides of Oswald's hands got warm and wet, and his nose was cold like a dog's, and his ears were burning hot.

The girls said afterwards that they shivered with terror, and their teeth chattered, but we did not see or hear this at the time.

"Shall we open the window and call police?" said Dora; and then Oswald suddenly thought of something, and he breathed more freely and he said—

"I *know* it's not ghosts, and I don't believe it's robbers. I expect it's a stray cat got in when the coals came this morning, and she's been hiding in the cellar, and now she's moving about. Let's go down and see."

The girls wouldn't, of course; but I could see that they breathed more freely too. But Dicky said, "All right; I will if you will."

H. O. said, "Do you think it's *really* a cat?" So we said he had better stay with the girls. And of course after that we had to let him and Alice both come. Dora said if we took

Noël down with his cold she would scream "Fire!" and "Murder!" and she didn't mind if the whole street heard.

So Noël agreed to be getting his clothes on, and the rest of us said we would go down and look for the cat.

Now Oswald *said* that about the cat, and it made it easier to go down, but in his inside he did not feel at all sure that it might not be robbers after all. Of course, we had often talked about robbers before, but it is very different when you sit in a room and listen and listen and listen; and Oswald felt somehow that it would be easier to go down and see what it was, than to wait, and listen, and wait, and wait, and listen, and wait, and then perhaps to hear *It*, whatever it was, come creeping slowly up the stairs as softly as *It* could with *Its* boots off, and the stairs creaking, towards the room where we were with the door open in case of Eliza coming back suddenly, and all dark on the landings. And then it would have been just as bad, and it would have lasted longer, and you would have known you were a coward besides. Dicky says he felt all these same things. Many people would say we were young heroes to go down as we did; so I have tried to explain, because no young hero wishes to have more credit than he deserves.

The landing gas was turned down low—just a blue bead —and we four went out very softly, wrapped in our blankets, and we stood on the top of the stairs a good long time before we began to go down. And we listened and listened till our ears buzzed.

And Oswald whispered to Dicky, and Dicky went into our room and fetched the large toy pistol that is a foot long, and that has the trigger broken, and I took it because I am the eldest; and I don't think either of us thought it was the cat now. But Alice and H. O. did. Dicky got the poker out of Noël's room, and told Dora it was to settle the cat with when we caught her.

Then Oswald whispered, "Let's play at burglars; Dicky and I are armed to the teeth, we will go first. You keep a flight behind us, and be a reinforcement if we are attacked. Or you can retreat and defend the women and children in the fortress, if you'd rather."

But they said they would be a reinforcement.

Oswald's teeth chattered a little when he spoke. It was not with anything else except cold.

So Dicky and Oswald crept down, and when we got to the bottom of the stairs, we saw Father's study door just ajar, and the crack of light. And Oswald was so pleased to see the light, knowing that burglars prefer the dark, or at any rate the dark lantern, that he felt really sure it *was* the cat after all, and then he thought it would be fun to make the others upstairs think it was really a robber. So he cocked the pistol—you can cock it, but it doesn't go off—and he said, "Come on, Dick!" and he rushed at the study door and burst into the room, crying, "Surrender! you are discovered! Surrender, or I fire! Throw up your hands!"

And, as he finished saying it, he saw before him, standing on the study hearthrug, a Real Robber. There was no mistake about it. Oswald was sure it was a robber, because it had a screwdriver in its hands, and was standing near the cupboard door that H. O. broke the lock off, and there were gimlets and screws and things on the floor. There is nothing in that cupboard but old ledgers and magazines and the tool chest, but, of course, a robber could not know that beforehand.

When Oswald saw that there really was a robber, and that he was so heavily armed with the screwdriver, he did not feel comfortable. But he kept the pistol pointed at the robber, and—you will hardly believe it, but it is true—the robber threw down the screwdriver clattering on the other tools, and he *did* throw up his hands, and said—

"I surrender; don't shoot me! How many of you are there?"

So Dicky said, "You are outnumbered. Are you armed?"

And the robber said, "No, not in the least."

And Oswald said, still pointing the pistol, and feeling very strong and brave and as if he was in a book, "Turn out your pockets."

The robber did: and while he turned them out, we looked at him. He was of the middle height, and clad in a black frock-coat and grey trousers. His boots were a little gone at the sides, and his shirt-cuffs were a bit frayed, but otherwise he was of gentlemanly demeanour. He had a thin, wrinkled face, with big, light eyes that sparkled, and then looked soft very queerly, and a short beard. In his youth it must have been of a fair golden colour, but now it was tinged with grey. Oswald was sorry for him, especially when he saw that one of his pockets had a large hole in it, and that he had nothing in his pockets but letters and string and three boxes of matches, and a pipe and a handkerchief and a thin tobacco pouch and two pennies. We made him put all the things on the table, and then he said—

"Well, you've caught me; what are you going to do with me? Police?"

Alice and H. O. had come down to be reinforcements, when they heard a shout, and when Alice saw that it was a Real Robber, and that he had surrendered, she clapped her hands and said, "Bravo, boys!" and so did H. O. And now she said, "If he gives his word of honour not to escape, I shouldn't call the police: it seems a pity. Wait till Father comes home."

The robber agreed to this, and gave his word of honour, and asked if he might put on a pipe, and we said "Yes," and he sat in Father's armchair and warmed his boots, which steamed, and I sent H. O. and Alice to put on some clothes and tell the others, and bring down Dicky's and my knicker-bockers, and the rest of the chestnuts.

And they all came, and we sat round the fire, and it was jolly. The robber was very friendly, and talked to us a great deal.

"I wasn't always in this low way of business," he said, when Noël said something about the things he had turned out of his pockets. "It's a great come-down to a man like me. But, if I must be caught, it's something to be caught by brave young heroes like you. My stars! How you did bolt into the room,—'Surrender, and up with your hands!' You might have been born and bred to the thief-catching."

Oswald is sorry if it was mean, but he could not own up just then that he did not think there was any one in the study when he did that brave if rash act. He has told since.

"And what made you think there was any one in the house?" the robber asked, when he had thrown his head back, and laughed for quite half a minute. So we told him. And he applauded our valour, and Alice and H. O. explained that they would have said "Surrender," too, only they were reinforcements.

The robber ate some of the chestnuts—and we sat and wondered when Father would come home, and what he would say to us for our intrepid conduct. And the robber told us of all the things he had done before he began to break into houses. Dicky picked up the tools from the floor, and suddenly he said—

"Why, this is Father's screwdriver and his gimlets, and all! Well, I do call it jolly cheek to pick a man's locks with his own tools!"

"True, true," said the robber. "It is cheek, of the jolliest! But you see I've come down in the world. I was a highway robber once, but horses are so expensive to hire—five shillings an hour, you know—and I couldn't afford to keep them. The highwayman business isn't what it was."

"What about a bike?" said H. O.

But the robber thought cycles were low—and besides you couldn't go across country with them when occasion arose, as you could with a trusty steed. And he talked of highwaymen as if he knew just how we liked hearing it.

Then he told us how he had been a pirate captain—and how he had sailed over waves mountains high, and gained rich prizes—and how he *did* begin to think that here he had found a profession to his mind.

"I don't say there are no ups and downs in it," he said, "especially in stormy weather. But what a trade! And a sword at your side, and the Jolly Roger flying at the peak, and a prize in sight. And all the black mouths of your guns pointed at the laden trader—and the wind in your favour, and your trusty crew ready to live and die for you! Oh— but it's a grand life!"

I did feel so sorry for him. He used such nice words, and he had a gentleman's voice.

"I'm sure you weren't brought up to be a pirate," said Dora. She had dressed even to her collar—and made Noël do it too—but the rest of us were in blankets with just a few odd things put on anyhow underneath.

The robber frowned and sighed.

"No," he said. "I was brought up to the law. I was at Balliol, bless your hearts, and that's true anyway." He sighed again, and looked hard at the fire.

"That was my Father's college," H. O. was beginning, but Dicky said—

"Why did you leave off being a pirate?"

"A pirate?" he said, as if he had not been thinking of such things. "Oh, yes; why I gave it up because—because I could not get over the dreadful sea-sickness."

"Nelson was sea-sick," said Oswald.

"Ah," said the robber; "but I hadn't his luck or his pluck, or something. He stuck to it and won Trafalgar, didn't he? 'Kiss me, Hardy'—and all that, eh? *I* couldn't stick to it—I had to resign. And nobody kissed *me*."

I saw by his understanding about Nelson that he was really a man who had been to a good school as well as to Balliol.

Then we asked him, "And what did you do then?"

And Alice asked if he was ever a coiner, and we told him how we had thought we'd caught the desperate gang next door, and he was very much interested and said he was glad he had never taken to coining. "Besides, the coins are so ugly nowadays," he said, "no one could really find any pleasure in making them. And it's a hole-and-corner business at the best, isn't it?—and it must be a very thirsty one—with the hot metal and furnaces and things."

And again he looked at the fire.

Oswald forgot for a minute that the interesting stranger was a robber, and asked him if he wouldn't have a drink. Oswald has heard Father do this to his friends, so he knows it is the right thing. The robber said he didn't mind if he did. And that is right, too.

And Dora went and got a bottle of Father's ale—the Light Sparkling Family—and a glass, and we gave it to the robber. Dora said she would be responsible.

Then when he had had a drink he told us about bandits, but he said it was so bad in wet weather. Bandits' caves were hardly ever properly weathertight. And bush-ranging was the same.

"As a matter of fact," he said, "I was bush-ranging this afternoon, among the furze-bushes on the Heath, but I had no luck. I stopped the Lord Mayor in his gilt coach, with all his footmen in plush and gold lace, smart as cockatoos.

But it was no go. The Lord Mayor hadn't a stiver in his pockets. One of the footmen had six new pennies: the Lord Mayor always pays his servants' wages in new pennies. I spent fourpence of that in bread and cheese, that on the table's the tuppence. Ah, it's a poor trade!" And then he filled his pipe again.

We had turned out the gas, so that Father should have a jolly good surprise when he did come home, and we sat and talked as pleasant as could be. I never liked a new man better than I liked that robber. And I felt so sorry for him. He told us he had been a war-correspondent and an editor, in happier days, as well as a horse-stealer and a colonel of dragoons.

And quite suddenly, just as we were telling him about Lord Tottenham and our being highwaymen ourselves, he put up his hand and said "Shish!" and we were quiet and listened.

There was a scrape, scrape, scraping noise; it came from downstairs.

"They're filing something," whispered the robber, "here —shut up, give me that pistol, and the poker. There *is* a buglar now, and no mistake."

"It's only a toy one and it won't go off," I said, "but you can cock it."

Then we heard a snap.

"There goes the window bar," said the robber softly. "Jove! what an adventure! You kids stay here, I'll tackle it."

But Dicky and I said we should come. So he let us go as far as the bottom of the kitchen stairs, and we took the tongs and shovel with us. There was a light in the kitchen; a very little light. It is curious we never thought, any of us, that this might be a plant of our robber's to get away. We never thought of doubting his word of honour. And we were right.

That noble robber dashed the kitchen door open, and

rushed in with the big toy pistol in one hand and the poker in the other, shouting out just like Oswald had done—

"Surrender! You are discovered! Surrender, or I'll fire! Throw up your hands!" And Dicky and I rattled the tongs and shovel so that he might know there were more of us, all bristling with weapons.

And we heard a husky voice in the kitchen saying—

"All right, governor! Stow that scent sprinkler. I'll give in. Blowed if I ain't pretty well sick of the job, anyway."

Then we went in. Our robber was standing in the grandest manner with his legs very wide apart, and the pistol pointing at the cowering burglar. The burglar was a large man who did not mean to have a beard, I think, but he had got some of one, and a red comforter, and a fur cap, and his face was red and his voice was thick. How different from our own robber! The burglar had a dark lantern, and he was standing by the plate-basket. When we had lit the gas we all thought he was very like what a burglar ought to be. He did not look as if he could ever have been a priate or a highwayman, or anything really dashing or noble, and he scowled and shuffled his feet and said: "Well, go on; why don't yer fetch the pleece?"

"Upon my word, I don't know," said our robber, rubbing his chin. "Oswald, why don't we fetch the police?"

It is not every robber that I would stand Christian names from, I can tell you; but just then I didn't think of that. I just said—

"Do you mean I'm to fetch one?"

Our robber looked at the burglar and said nothing.

Then the burglar began to speak very fast, and to look different ways with his hard, shiny little eyes.

"Lookee 'ere, governor," he said, "I was stony broke, so help me, I was. And blessed if I've nicked a ha'porth of your little lot. You know yourself there ain't much to tempt a bloke," he shook the plate-basket as if he was angry with it, and the yellowy spoons and forks rattled. "I was just a-looking through this 'ere Bank-ollerday show, when you come. Let me off, sir. Come now, I've got kids of my own at home, strike me if I ain't—same as yours—I've got a nipper just about 'is size, and what'll come of them if I'm lagged? I ain't been in it long, sir, and I ain't 'andy at it."

"No," said our robber; "you certainly are not."

Alice and the others had come down by now to see what was happening. Alice told me afterwards they thought it really was the cat this time.

"No, I ain't 'andy, as you say, sir, and if you let me off this once I'll chuck the whole blooming bizz; take my civvy, I will. Don't be hard on a cove, mister; think of the missis and the kids. I've got one just the cut of little missy there; bless 'er pretty 'eart."

"Your family certainly fits your circumstances very nicely," said our robber.

Then Alice said—

"Oh, do let him go! If he's got a little girl like me, whatever will she do? Suppose it was Father!"

"I don't think he's got a little girl like you, my dear," said our robber, "and I think he'll be safer under lock and key."

"You ask yer Father to let me go, miss," said the burglar; "'e won't 'ave the 'art to refuse you."

"If I do," said Alice, "will you promise never to come back?"

"Not me, miss," the burglar said very earnestly, and he looked at the plate-basket again, as if that alone would be enough to keep him away, our robber said afterwards.

"And will you be good and not rob any more?" said Alice.

"I'll turn over a noo leaf, miss, so help me."

Then Alice said—

"Oh, do let him go! I'm sure he'll be good."

But our robber said no, it wouldn't be right; we must wait till Father came home.

Then H. O. said, very suddenly and plainly:

"I don't think it's at all fair, when you're a robber yourself."

The minute he'd said it the burglar said, "Kidded, by gum!"—and then our robber made a step towards him to catch hold of him, and before you had time to think "Hullo!" the burglar knocked the pistol up with one hand and knocked our robber down with the other, and was off out of the window like a shot, though Oswald and Dicky did try to stop him by holding on to his legs.

And that burglar had the cheek to put his head in at the window and say, "I'll give yer love to the kids and the missis"—and he was off like winking, and there were Alice and Dora trying to pick up our robber, and asking him whether he was hurt and where. He wasn't hurt at all, except a lump at the back of his head. And he got up, and we dusted the kitchen floor off him. Eliza is a dirty girl.

Then he said, "Let's put up the shutters. It never rains but it pours. Now you've had two burglars I daresay you'll have twenty." So we put up the shutters, which Eliza has strict orders to do before she goes out, only she never does, and we went back to Father's study, and the robber said, "What a night we are having!" and put his boots back in the fender to go on steaming, and then we all talked at once. It was the most wonderful adventure we ever had, though it wasn't treasure-seeking—at least not ours. I suppose it was the burglar's treasure-seeking, but he didn't get much—and our robber said he didn't believe a word about those kids that were so like Alice and me.

And then there was the click of the gate, and we said, "Here's Father," and the robber said, "And now for the police,"

Then we all jumped up. We did like him so much, and it seemed so unfair that he should be sent to prison, and the horrid, lumping big burglar not.

And Alice said, "Oh, *no*—run! Dicky will let you out at the back door. Oh, do go, go *now*."

And we all said, "Yes, *go*," and pulled him towards the door, and gave him his hat and stick and the things out of his pockets.

But Father's latchkey was in the door, and it was too late.

Father came in quickly, purring with the cold, and began to say, "It's all right, Foulkes, I've got——" And then he stopped short and stared at us. Then he said, in the voice we all hate, "Children, what is the meaning of all this?"

And for a minute nobody spoke.

Then my Father said, "Foulkes, I must really apologise for these very naughty——"

And then our robber rubbed his hands and laughed, and cried out: "You're mistaken, my dear sir, I'm not Foulkes; I'm a robber, captured by these young people in the most gallant manner, 'Hands up, surrender, or I fire,' and all the rest of it. My word, Bastable, but you've got some kids worth having! I wish my Denny had their pluck."

Then we began to understand, and it was like being knocked down, it was so sudden. And our robber told us he wasn't a robber after all. He was only an old college friend of my Father's, and he had come after dinner, when Father was just trying to mend the lock H. O. had broken, to ask Father to get him a letter to a doctor about his little boy Denny, who was ill. And Father had gone over the Heath to Vanbrugh Park to see some rich people he knows and get the letter. And he had left Mr. Foulkes to wait till he came back, because it was important to know at once whether Father could get the letter, and if he couldn't Mr. Foulkes would have had to try some one else directly.

We were dumb with amazement.

Our robber told my Father about the other burglar, and said he was sorry he'd let him escape, but my Father said, "Oh, it's all right: poor beggar; if he really had kids at home: you never can tell—forgive us our debts, don't you know; but tell me about the first business. It must have been moderately entertaining."

Then our robber told my Father how I had rushed into the room with a pistol, crying out... but you know all about that. And he laid it on so thick and fat about plucky young 'uns, and chips of old blocks, and things like that, that I felt I was purple with shame, even under the blanket. So I swallowed that thing that tries to prevent you speaking when you ought to, and I said, "Look here, Father, I didn't really think there was anyone in the study. We thought it was a cat at first, and then I thought there was no one there, and I was just larking. And when I said surrender and all that, it was just the game, don't you know?"

Then our robber said, "Yes, old chap; but when you found there really *was* some one there, you dropped the pistol and bunked, didn't you, eh?"

And I said, "No; I thought 'Hullo! here's a robber! Well, it's all up, I suppose, but I may as well hold on and see what happens.'"

And I was glad I'd owned up, for Father slapped me on the back, and said I was a young brick, and our robber said I was no funk anyway, and though I got very hot under the blanket I liked it, and I explained that the others would have done the same if they had thought of it.

Then Father got up some more beer, and laughed about Dora's responsibility, and he got out a box of figs he had bought for us, only he hadn't given it to us because of the Water Rates, and Eliza came in and brought up the bread and cheese, and what there was left of the neck of mutton

—cold wreck of mutton, Father called it—and we had a feast—like a picnic—all sitting anywhere, and eating with our fingers. It was prime. We sat up till past twelve o'clock, and I never felt so pleased to think I was not born a girl. It was hard on the others; they would have done just the same if they'd thought of it. But it does make you feel jolly when your pater says you're a young brick!

When Mr. Foulkes was going, he said to Alice, "Good-bye, Hardy."

And Alice understood, of course, and kissed him as hard as she could.

And she said, "I wanted to, when you said no one kissed you when you left off being a pirate captain."

And he said, "I know you did, my dear."

And Dora kissed him too, and said, "I suppose none of these tales were true?"

And our robber just said, "I tried to play the part properly, my dear."

And he jolly well did play it, and no mistake. We have often seen him since, and his boy Denny, and his girl Daisy, but that comes in another story.

And if any of you kids who read this ever had two such adventures in one night you can just write and tell me. That's all.

CHAPTER XIV

THE DIVINING-ROD

YOU HAVE no idea how uncomfortable the house was on the day when we sought for gold with the divining-rod. It was like a spring-cleaning in the winter-time. All the carpets were up, because Father had told Eliza to make the place decent as there was a gentleman coming to dinner the next day. So she got in a charwoman, and they slopped water about, and left brooms and brushes on the stairs for people to tumble over. H. O. got a big bump on his head in that way, and when he said it was too bad, Eliza said he should keep in the nursery then, and not be where he'd no business. We bandaged his head with a towel, and then he stopped crying and played at being England's wounded hero dying in the cockpit, while every man was doing his duty, as the hero had told them to, and Alice was Hardy, and I was the doctor, and the others were the crew. Playing at Hardy made us think of our own dear robber, and we wished he was there, and wondered if we should ever see him any more.

We were rather astonished at Father's having any one to dinner, because now he never seems to think of anything but business. Before Mother died people often came to dinner, and Father's business did not take up so much of his time and was not the bother it is now. And we used to see who could go furthest down in our nightgowns and get nice things to eat, without being seen, out of the dishes as they came out of the dining-room. Eliza can't cook very nice things. She told Father she was a good plain cook, but he says it was a fancy portrait. We stayed in the nursery until the charwoman came in and told us to be off—she was going to make one job of it, and have our carpet up as well as all the others, now the man was here to beat them. It came up, and it was very dusty—and under it we found my threepenny-bit that I lost ages ago, which shows what Eliza is. H. O. had got tired of being the wounded hero, and Dicky was so tired of doing nothing that Dora said she knew he'd begin to tease Noël in a minute; then of course Dicky said he wasn't going to tease anybody—he was going out to the Heath. He said he'd heard that nagging women drove a man from his home, and now he'd found it was quite true. Oswald always tries to be a peace-maker, so he told Dicky to shut up and not make an ass of himself. And Alice said, "Well, Dora began——" and Dora tossed her chin up and said it wasn't any business of Oswald's any way, and no one asked Alice's opinion. So we all felt very uncomfortable till Noël said, "Don't let's quarrel about nothing. You know let dogs delight—and I made up another piece while you were talking—

> Quarrelling is an evil thing,
> It fills with gall life's cup;
> For when once you begin
> It takes such a long time to make it up."

We all laughed then and stopped jawing at each other. Noël is very funny with his poetry. But that piece happened to come out quite true. You begin to quarrel and then you can't stop; often, long before the others are ready to cry and make it up, I see how silly it is, and I want to laugh; but it doesn't do to say so—for it only makes the others crosser than they were before. I wonder why that is?

Alice said Noël ought to be poet laureate, and she actually went out in the cold and got some laurel leaves—the spotted kind—out of the garden, and Dora made a crown and we put it on him. He was quite pleased; but the leaves made a mess, and Eliza said, "Don't." I believe that's a word grown-ups use more than any other. Then suddenly Alice thought of that old idea of hers for finding treasure, and she said—

"Do let's try the divining-rod."

So Oswald said, "Fair priestess, we do greatly desire to find gold beneath our land, therefore we pray thee practise with the divining-rod, and tell us where we can find it."

"Do ye desire to fashion it of helms and hauberks?" said Alice.

"Yes," said Noël; "and chains and ouches."

"I bet you don't know what an 'ouch' is," said Dicky.

"Yes I do, so there!" said Noël. "It's a carcanet. I looked it out in the dicker, now then!"

We asked him what a carcanet was, but he wouldn't say.

"And we want to make fair goblets of the gold," said Oswald.

"Yes, to drink coconut milk out of," said H. O.

"And we desire to build fair palaces of it," said Dicky.

"And to buy things," said Dora; "a great many things. New Sunday frocks and hats and kid gloves and——"

She would have gone on for ever so long only we reminded her that we hadn't found the gold yet.

By this Alice had put on the nursery tablecloth, which is green, and tied the old blue and yellow antimacassar over her head, and she said—

"If your intentions are correct, fear nothing and follow me."

And she went down into the hall. We all followed chanting "Heroes." It is a gloomy thing the girls learnt at the High School, and we always use it when we want a priestly chant.

Alice stopped short by the hat-stand, and held up her hands as well as she could for the table-cloth, and said—

We followed her on tiptoe, and Alice sang as she went

"Now, great altar of the golden idol, yield me the divining-rod that I may use it for the good of the suffering people."

The umbrella-stand was the altar of the golden idol, and it yielded her the old school umbrella. She carried it between her palms.

"Now," she said, "I shall sing the magic chant. You mustn't say anything, but just follow wherever I go—like follow my leader, you know—and when there is gold underneath the magic rod will twist in the hand of the priestess like a live thing that seeks to be free. Then you will dig, and the golden treasure will be revealed. H. O., if you make that clatter with your boots they'll come and tell us not to. Now come on all of you."

So she went upstairs and down and into every room. We followed her on tiptoe, and Alice sang as she went. What she sang is not out of a book—Noël made it up while she was dressing up for the priestess.

> Ashen rod cold
> That here I hold,
> Teach me where to find the gold.

When we came to where Eliza was, she said, "Get along with you"; but Dora said it was only a game, and we wouldn't touch anything, and our boots were quite clean, and Eliza might as well let us. So she did.

It was all right for the priestess, but it was a little dull for the rest of us, because she wouldn't let us sing too; so we said we'd had enough of it, and if she couldn't find the gold we'd leave off and play something else. The priestess said, "All right, wait a minute," and went on singing. Then we all followed her back into the nursery, where the carpet was up and the boards smelt of soft soap. Then she said, "It moves, it moves! Once more the choral hymn!" So we sang

"See the rich treasure!"

"Heroes" again, and in the middle the umbrella dropped from her hands.

"The magic rod has spoken," said Alice; "dig here, and that with courage and despatch." We didn't quite see how to dig, but we all began to scratch on the floor with our hands, but the priestess said, "Don't be so silly! It's the place where they come to do the gas. The board's loose. Dig an you value your lives, for ere sundown the dragon who guards this spoil will return in his fiery fury and make you his unresisting prey."

So we dug—that is, we got the loose board up. And Alice threw up her arms and cried—

"See the rich treasure—the gold in thick layers, with silver and diamonds stuck in it!"

"Like currants in cake," said H. O.

"It's a lovely treasure," said Dicky yawning. "Let's come back and carry it away another day."

But Alice was kneeling by the hole.

"Let me feast my eyes on the golden splendour," she said, "hidden these long centuries from the human eye. Behold how the magic rod has led us to treasures more—Oswald don't push so!—more bright than ever monarch—— I say there *is* something down there really. I saw it shine!"

We thought she was kidding, but when she began to try to get into the hole, which was much too small, we saw she meant it, so I said, "Let's have a squint," and I looked, but I couldn't see anything, even when I lay down on my stomach. The others lay down on their stomachs too and tried to see, all but Noël, who stood and looked at us and said we were the great serpents come down to drink at the magic pool. He wanted to be the knight and slay the great serpents with his good sword—he even drew the umbrella ready—but Alice said, "All right, we will in a minute. But now—I'm sure I saw it; do get a match, Noël, there's a dear,"

"What did you see?" asked Noël, beginning to go for the matches very slowly.

"Something bright, away in the corner under the board against the beam."

"Perhaps it was a rat's eye," Noël said, "or a snake's," and we did not put our heads quite so close to the hole till he came back with the matches.

Then I struck a match, and Alice cried, "There it is!"

And there it was, and it was a half-sovereign, partly dusty and partly bright. We think perhaps a mouse, disturbed by the carpets being taken up, may have brushed the dust of years from part of the half-sovereign with his tail. We can't imagine how it came there, only Dora thinks she remembers once when H. O. was very little Mother gave him some money to hold, and he dropped it, and it rolled all over the floor. So we think perhaps this was part of it. We were very glad. H. O. wanted to go out at once and buy a mask he had seen for fourpence. It had been a shilling mask, but now it was going very cheap because Guy Fawkes' Day was over, and it was a little cracked at the top. But Dora said, "I don't know that it's our money. Let's wait and ask Father."

But H. O. did not care about waiting, and I felt for him. Dora is rather like grown-ups in that way; she does not seem to understand that when you want a thing you do want it, and that you don't wish to wait, even a minute.

So we went and asked Albert-next-door's uncle. He was pegging away at one of the rotten novels he has to write to make his living, but he said we weren't interrupting him at all.

"My hero's folly has involved him in a difficulty," he said. "It is his own fault. I will leave him to meditate on the incredible fatuity—the hare-brained recklessness—which have brought him to this pass. It will be a lesson to him. I, mean-

"Let the Priestess set forth the tale in fitting speech"

time, will give myself unreservedly to the pleasures of your conversation."

That's one thing I like Albert's uncle for. He always talks like a book, and yet you can always understand what he means. I think he is more like us, inside of his mind, than most grown-up people are. He can pretend beautifully. I never met anyone else so good at it, except our robber, and we began it, with him. But it was Albert's uncle who first taught us how to make people talk like books when you're playing things, and he made us learn to tell a story straight from the beginning, not starting in the middle like most people do. So now Oswald remembered what he had been told, as he generally does, and began at the beginning, but when he came to where Alice said she was the priestess, Albert's uncle said—

"Let the priestess herself set forth the tale in fitting speech."

So Alice said, "O high priest of the great idol, the humblest of thy slaves took the school umbrella for a divining-rod, and sang the song of inver—what's-it's-name?"

"Invocation perhaps?" said Albert's uncle.

"Yes; and then I went about and about and the others got tired, so the divining-rod fell on a certain spot, and I said, 'Dig,' and we dug—it was where the loose board is for the gas men—and then there really and truly was a half-sovereign lying under the boards, and here it is."

Albert's uncle took it and looked at it.

"The great high priest will bite it to see if it's good," he said, and he did. "I congratulate you," he went on; "you are indeed among those favoured by the Immortals. First you find half-crowns in the garden, and now this. The high priest advises you to tell your Father, and ask if you may keep it. My hero has become penitent, but impatient. I must pull him out of this scrape. Ye have my leave to depart."

Of course we know from Kipling that that means, "You'd better bunk, and be sharp about it," so we came away. I do like Albert's uncle. I shall be like that when I'm a man. He gave us our Jungle books, and he is awfully clever, though he does have to write grown-up tales.

We told Father about it that night. He was very kind. He said we might certainly have the half-sovereign, and he hoped we should enjoy ourselves with our treasure-trove.

Then he said, "Your dear Mother's Indian Uncle is coming to dinner here to-morrow night. So will you not drag the furniture about overhead, please, more than you're absolutely obliged; and H. O. might wear slippers or something. I can always distinguish the note of H. O.'s boots."

We said we would be very quiet, and Father went on—

"This Indian uncle is not used to children, and he is coming to talk business with me. It is really important that he should be quiet. Do you think, Dora, that perhaps bed at six for H. O. and Noël——"

But H. O. said, "Father, I really and truly won't make a noise. I'll stand on my head all the evening sooner than disturb the Indian Uncle with my boots."

And Alice said Noël never made a row anyhow.

So Father laughed and said, "All right." And he said we might do as we liked with the half-sovereign. "Only for goodness' sake don't try to go in for business with it," he said. "It's always a mistake to go into business with an insufficient capital."

We talked it over all that evening, and we decided that as we were not to go into business with our half-sovereign it was no use not spending it at once, and so we might as well have a right royal feast. The next day we went out and bought the things. We got figs, and almonds and raisins, and a real raw rabbit, and Eliza promised to cook it for us if we would wait till to-morrow, because of the Indian Uncle coming to dinner. She was very busy cooking nice things for him to eat. We got the rabbit because we are so tired of beef and mutton, and Father hasn't a bill at the poultry shop. And we got some flowers to go on the dinner-table for Father's party. And we got hardbake and raspberry noyau and peppermint rock and oranges and a coconut, with other nice things. We put it all in the top long drawer. It is H. O.'s play drawer, and we made him turn his things out and put them in Father's old portmanteau. H. O. is getting old enough now to learn to be unselfish, and besides, his drawer wanted tidying very badly. Then we all vowed by the honour of the ancient House of Bastable that we would not touch any of the feast till Dora gave the word next day. And we gave H. O. some of the hardbake, to make it easier for him to keep his vow. The next day was the most rememorable day in all our lives, but we didn't know that then. But that is another story. I think that is such a useful way to know when you can't think how to end up a chapter. I learnt it from another writer named Kipling. I've mentioned him before, I believe, but he deserves it!

CHAPTER XV

"LO, THE POOR INDIAN!"

IT WAS all very well for Father to ask us not to make a row because the Indian Uncle was coming to talk business, but my young brother's boots are not the only things that make a noise. We took his boots away and made him wear Dora's bath slippers, which are soft and woolly, and hardly any soles to them; and of course we wanted to see the Uncle, so we looked over the banisters when he came, and we were as quiet as mice—but when Eliza had let him in she went straight down to the kitchen and made the most awful row you ever heard, it sounded like the Day of Judgment, or all the saucepans and crockery in the house being kicked about the floor, but she told me afterwards it was only the tea-tray and one or two cups and saucers, that she had knocked over in her flurry. We heard the Uncle say, "God bless my soul!" and then he went into Father's study and the door was shut—we didn't see him properly at all that time.

I don't believe the dinner was very nice. Something got burned I'm sure—for we smelt it. It was an extra smell, besides the mutton. I know *that* got burned. Eliza wouldn't have any of us in the kitchen except Dora—till dinner was over. Then we got what was left of the dessert, and had it on the stairs—just round the corner where they can't see you from the hall, unless the first landing gas is lighted. Suddenly the study door opened and the Uncle came out and went and felt in his greatcoat pocket. It was his cigar-case he wanted. We saw that afterwards. We got a much better view of him then. He didn't look like an Indian but just like

We were looking over the banisters

a kind of brown, big Englishman, and of course he didn't
see us, but we heard him mutter to himself—

"Shocking bad dinner! Eh!—what?" When he went back
to the study he didn't shut the door properly. That door has
always been a little tiresome since the day we took the lock
off to get out the pencil sharpener H. O. had shoved into the
keyhole. We didn't listen—really and truly—but the Indian
Uncle has a very big voice, and Father was not going to be
beaten by a poor Indian in talking or anything else—so he
spoke up too, like a man, and I heard him say it was a very
good business, and only wanted a little capital—and he said
it as if it was an imposition he had learned, and he hated
having to say it. The Uncle said, "Pooh, pooh!" to that, and
then he said he was afraid that what that same business
wanted was not capital but management. Then I heard my
Father say, "It is not a pleasant subject: I am sorry I introduced it. Suppose we change it, sir. Let me fill your glass."
Then the poor Indian said something about vintage—and
that a poor, broken-down man like he was couldn't be too
careful. And then Father said, "Well, whisky then," and
afterwards they talked about Native Races and Imperial
something or other and it got very dull.

So then Oswald remembered that you must not hear
what people do not intend you to hear—even if you are not
listening; and he said, "We ought not to stay here any longer.
Perhaps they would not like us to hear——"

Alice said, "Oh, do you think it could possibly matter?"
and went and shut the study door softly but quite tight. So
it was no use staying there any longer, and we went to the
nursery.

Then Noël said, "Now I understand. Of course my
Father is making a banquet for the Indian, because he is a poor,
broken-down man. We might have known that from 'Lo,
the poor Indian!' you know."

We all agreed with him, and we were glad to have the thing explained, because we had not understood before what Father wanted to have people to dinner for—and not let us come in.

"Poor people are very proud," said Alice, "and I expect Father thought the Indian would be ashamed, if all of us children knew how poor he was."

Then Dora said, "Poverty is no disgrace. We should honour honest Poverty."

And we all agreed that that was so.

"I wish his dinner had not been so nasty," Dora said, while Oswald put lumps of coal on the fire with his fingers, so as not to make a noise. He is a very thoughtful boy, and he did not wipe his fingers on his trouser leg as perhaps Noël or H. O. would have done, but he just rubbed them on Dora's handkerchief while she was talking. "I am afraid the dinner was horrid." Dora went on. "The table looked very nice with the flowers we got. I set it myself, and Eliza made me borrow the silver spoons and forks from Albert-next-door's Mother."

"I hope the poor Indian is honest," said Dicky gloomily, "when you are a poor, broken-down man silver spoons must be a great temptation."

Oswald told him not to talk such tommy-rot because the Indian was a relation, so of course he couldn't do anything dishonourable. And Dora said it was all right any way, because she had washed up the spoons and forks herself and counted them and they were all there, and she had put them into their wash-leather bag and taken them back to Albert-next-door's Mother.

"And the brussels sprouts were all wet and swimmy," she went on, "and the potatoes looked grey—and there were bits of black in the gravy—and the mutton was bluey-red and soft in the middle. I saw it when it came out. The apple-pie looked very nice—but it wasn't quite done in the apple part. The other thing that was burnt—you must have smelt it, it was the soup."

"It is a pity," said Oswald; "I don't suppose he gets a good dinner every day."

"No more do we," said H. O., "but we shall to-morrow."

I thought of all the things we had bought with our half-sovereign—the rabbit and the sweets and the almonds and raisins and figs and the coconut: and I thought of the nasty mutton and things, and while I was thinking about it all, Alice said—

"Let's ask the poor Indian to come to dinner with *us* to-morrow." I should have said it myself if she had given me time.

We got the little ones to go to bed by promising to put a note on their dressing-table saying what had happened, so that they might know first thing in the morning, or in the middle of the night if they happened to wake up, and then we elders arranged everything.

I waited by the back door, and when the Uncle was beginning to go Dicky was to drop a marble down between the banisters for a signal, so that I could run round and meet the Uncle as he came out.

This seems like deceit, but if you are a thoughtful and considerate boy you will understand that we could not go down and say to the Uncle in the hall under Father's eye, "Father has given you a beastly, nasty dinner, but if you will come to dinner with us to-morrow, we will show you our idea of good things to eat." You will see, if you think it over, that this would not have been at all polite to Father.

So when the Uncle left, Father saw him to the door and let him out, and then went back to the study, looking very sad, Dora says.

As the poor Indian came down our steps he saw me there

at the gate. I did not mind his being poor, and I said, "Good evening, Uncle," just as politely as though he had been about to ascend into one of the gilded chariots of the rich and affluent, instead of having to walk to the station a quarter of a mile in the mud, unless he had the money for a tram fare.

"Good evening, Uncle." I said it again, for he stood staring at me. I don't suppose he was used to politeness from boys —some boys are anything but—especially to the Aged Poor.

So I said, "Good evening, Uncle," yet once again. Then he said—

"Time you were in bed, young man. Eh!—what?"

Then I saw I must speak plainly with him, man to man. So I did. I said—

"You've been dining with my Father, and we couldn't help hearing you say the dinner was shocking. So we thought as you're an Indian, perhaps you're very poor"—I didn't like to tell him we had heard the dreadful truth from his own lips, so I went on, "because of 'Lo, the poor Indian'—you know—and you can't get a good dinner every day. And we are very sorry if you're poor; and won't you come and have dinner with us to-morrow—with us children, I mean? It's a very, very good dinner—rabbit, and hardbake, and coconut—and you needn't mind us knowing you're poor, because we know honourable poverty is no disgrace, and——" I could have gone on much longer, but he interrupted me to say—

"Upon my word! And what's *your* name, eh?"

"Oswald Bastable," I said; and I do hope you people who are reading this story have not guessed before that I was Oswald all the time.

"Oswald Bastable, eh? Bless my soul!" said the poor Indian. "Yes, I'll dine with you, Mr. Oswald Bastable, with all the pleasure in life. Very kind and cordial invitation, I'm sure. Good night, sir. At one o'clock, I presume?"

"Yes, at one," I said. "Good night, sir."

Then I went in and told the others, and we wrote a paper and put it on the boys' dressing-table, and it said—

"The poor Indian is coming at one. He seemed very grateful to me for my kindness."

We did not tell Father that the Uncle was coming to dinner with us, for the polite reason that I have explained before. But we had to tell Eliza; so we said a friend was coming to dinner and we wanted everything very nice. I think she thought it was Albert-next-door, but she was in a good temper that day, and she agreed to cook the rabbit and to make a pudding with currants in it. And when one o'clock came the Indian Uncle came too. I let him in and helped him off with his great-coat, which was all furry inside, and took him straight to the nursery. We were to have dinner there as usual, for we had decided from the first that he would enjoy himself more if he was not made a stranger of. We agreed to treat him as one of ourselves, because if we were too polite, he might think it was our pride because he was poor.

He shook hands with us all and asked our ages, and what schools we went to, and shook his head when we said we were having a holiday just now. I felt rather uncomfortable—I always do when they talk about schools—and I couldn't think of anything to say to show him we meant to treat him as one of ourselves. I did ask if he played cricket. He said he had not played lately. And then no one said anything till dinner came in. We had all washed our faces and hands and brushed our hair before he came in, and we all looked very nice, especially Oswald, who had had his hair cut that very morning. When Eliza had brought in the rabbit and gone out again, we looked at each other in silent despair, like in books. It seemed as if it were going to be just a dull dinner like the one the poor Indian had had the night before; only, of course, the things to eat would be nicer. Dicky kicked

Oswald under the table to make him say something—and he had his new boots on, too!—but Oswald did not kick back; then the Uncle asked—

"Do you carve, sir, or shall I?"

Suddenly Alice said—

"Would you like a grown-up dinner, Uncle, or play-dinner?"

He did not hesitate a moment, but said, "Play-dinner, by all means. Eh!—what?" and then we knew it was all right.

So we at once showed the Uncle how to be a dauntless hunter. The rabbit was the deer we had slain in the green forest with our trusty yew bows, and we toasted the joints of it, when the Uncle had carved it, on bits of firewood sharpened to a point. The Uncle's piece got a little burnt, but he said it was delicious, and he said game was always nicer when you had killed it yourself. When Eliza had taken away the rabbit bones and brought in the pudding, we waited till she had gone out and shut the door, and then we put the dish down on the floor and slew the pudding in the dish in the good old-fashioned way. It was a wild boar at bay, and very hard indeed to kill, even with forks. The Uncle was very fierce indeed with the pudding, and jumped and howled when he speared it, but when it came to his turn to be helped he said, "No, thank you; think of my liver. Eh!—what?"

But he had some almonds and raisins—when we had climbed to the top of the chest of drawers to pluck them from the boughs of the great trees; and he had a fig from the cargo that the rich merchants brought in their ship—the long drawer was the ship—and the rest of us had the sweets and the coconut. It was a very glorious and beautiful feast, and when it was over we said we hoped it was better than the dinner last night. And he said:

"I never enjoyed a dinner more." He was too polite to say

The Uncle was very fierce indeed with the pudding

what he really thought about Father's dinner. And we saw that though he might be poor, he was a true gentleman.

He smoked a cigar while we finished up what there was left to eat, and told us about tiger shooting and about elephants. We asked him about wigwams, and wampum, and moccasins, and beavers, but he did not seem to know, or else he was shy about talking of the wonders of his native land.

We liked him very much indeed, and when he was going at last, Alice nudged me, and I said—

"There's one and threepence farthing left out of our half-sovereign. Will you take it, please, because we do like you very much indeed, and we don't want it, really; and we would rather you had it." And I put the money into his hand.

"I'll take the threepenny-bit," he said, turning the money over and looking at it, "but I couldn't rob you of the rest. By the way, where did you get the money for this most royal spread—half a sovereign you said—Eh!—what?"

We told him all about the different ways we had looked for treasure, and when we had been telling some time he sat down, to listen better; and at last we told him how Alice had played at divining-rod, and how it really had found a half-sovereign. Then he said he would like to see her do it again. But we explained that the rod would only show gold and silver, and that we were quite sure there was no more gold in the house, because we happened to have looked very carefully.

"Well, silver, then," said he; "let's hide the plate-basket, and little Alice shall make the divining-rod find it. Eh!—what?"

"There isn't any silver in the plate-basket now," Dora said. "Eliza asked me to borrow the silver spoons and forks for your dinner last night from Albert-next-door's Mother. Father never notices, but she thought it would be nicer for you. Our own silver went to have the dents taken out; and I don't think Father could afford to pay the man for doing it, for the silver hasn't come back."

"Bless my soul!" said the Uncle again, looking at the hole in the big chair that we burnt when we had Guy Fawkes' Day indoors. "And how much pocket-money do you get? Eh!—what?"

"We don't have any now," said Alice; "but indeed we don't want the other shilling. We'd much rather you had it, wouldn't we?"

And the rest of us said "Yes." The Uncle wouldn't take it, but he asked a lot of questions, and at last he went away. And when he went he said—

"Well, youngsters, I've enjoyed myself very much. I shan't forget your kind hospitality. Perhaps the poor Indian may be in a position to ask you all to dinner some day."

Oswald said if he ever could we should like to come very much, but he was not to trouble to get such a nice dinner as ours, because we could do very well with cold mutton and rice pudding. We do not like these things, but Oswald knows how to behave. Then the poor Indian went away.

We had not got any treasure by this party, but we had had a very good time, and I am sure the Uncle enjoyed himself.

We were so sorry he was going that we could none of us eat much tea; but we did not mind, because we had pleased the poor Indian and enjoyed ourselves too. Besides, as Dora said, "A contented mind is a continual feast," so it did not matter about not wanting tea.

Only H. O. did not seem to think a continual feast was a contented mind, and Eliza gave him a powder in what was left of the red-currant jelly Father had for the nasty dinner.

But the rest of us were quite well, and I think it must have been the coconut with H. O. We hoped nothing had disagreed with the Uncle, but we never knew.

CHAPTER XVI

THE END OF
THE TREASURE-SEEKING

Now it is coming near the end of our treasure-seeking, and the end was so wonderful that now nothing is like it used to be. It is like as if our fortunes had been in an earth-quake, and after those, you know, everything comes out wrong-way up.

The day after the Uncle speared the pudding with us opened in gloom and sadness. But you never know. It was destined to be a day when things happened. Yet no sign of this appeared in the early morning. Then all was misery and upsetness. None of us felt quite well; I don't know why: and Father had one of his awful colds, so Dora persuaded him not to go to London, but to stay cosy and warm in the study, and she made him some gruel. She makes it better than Eliza does; Eliza's gruel is all little lumps, and when you suck them it is dry oatmeal inside.

We kept as quiet as we could, and I made H. O. do some lessons, like the G. B. had advised us to. But it was very dull. There are some days when you seem to have got to the end of all the things that could ever possibly happen to you, and you feel you will spend all the rest of your life doing dull things just the same way. Days like this are generally wet days. But, as I said, you never know.

Then Dicky said if things went on like this he should run away to sea, and Alice said she thought it would be rather nice to go into a convent. H. O. was a little disagreeable be-cause of the powder Eliza had given him, so he tried to read two books at once, one with each eye, just because Noël wanted one of the books, which was very selfish of him, so it only made his headache worse. H. O. is getting old enough to learn by experience that it is wrong to be selfish, and when he complained about his head Oswald told him whose fault it was, because I am older than he is, and it is my duty to show him where he is wrong. But he began to cry, and then Oswald had to cheer him up because of Father wanting to be quiet. So Oswald said—

"They'll eat H. O. if you don't look out!"

And Dora said Oswald was too bad.

Of course Oswald was not going to interfere again, so he went to look out of the window and see the trams go by, and by and by H. O. came and looked out too, and Oswald, who knows when to be generous and forgiving, gave him a piece of blue pencil and two nibs, as good as new, to keep.

As they were looking out at the rain splashing on the stones in the street they saw a four-wheeled cab come lumbering up from the way the station is. Oswald called out—

"Here comes the coach of the Fairy Godmother. It'll stop here, you see if it doesn't!"

So they all came to the window to look. Oswald had only said that about stopping and he was stricken with wonder and amaze when the cab really did stop. It had boxes on the top and knobby parcels sticking out of the window, and it was something like going away to the seaside and something like the gentleman who takes things about in a carriage with the wooden shutters up, to sell to the drapers' shops. The cabman got down and someone inside handed out ever so many parcels of different shapes and sizes, and the cabman stood holding them in his arms and grinning over them.

Dora said, "It is a pity some one doesn't tell him this isn't the house." And then from inside the cab some one put out a foot feeling for the step, like a tortoise's foot coming out from under his shell when you are holding him off the ground, and then a leg came and more parcels, and then Noël cried—

"It's the poor Indian!"

And it was.

Eliza opened the door, and we were all leaning over the banisters. Father heard the noise of parcels and boxes in the hall, and he came out without remembering how bad his cold was. If you do that yourself when you have a cold they call you careless and naughty. Then we heard the poor Indian say to Father—

"I say, Dick, I dined with your kids yesterday—as I daresay they've told you. Jolliest little cubs I ever saw! Why didn't you let me see them the other night? The eldest is the image of poor Janey—and as to young Oswald, he's a man! If he's not a man, I'm a nigger! Eh!—what? And Dick, I say, I shouldn't wonder if I could find a friend to put a bit into that business of yours—eh?"

Then he and Father went into the study and the door was shut—and we went down and looked at the parcels. Some were done up in old, dirty newspapers, and tied with bits of rag, and some were in brown paper and string from the shops, and there were boxes. We wondered if the Uncle had come to stay and this was his luggage, or whether it was to sell. Some of it smelt of spices, like merchandise—and one bundle Alice felt certain was a bale. We heard a hand on the knob of the study door after a bit, and Alice said—

"Fly!" and we all got away but H. O., and the Uncle caught him by the leg as he was trying to get upstairs after us.

"Peeping at the baggage, eh?" said the Uncle, and the rest of us came down because it would have been dishonourable to leave H. O. alone in a scrape, and we wanted to see what was in the parcels.

"I didn't touch," said H. O. "Are you coming to stay? I hope you are."

"No harm done if you did touch," said the good, kind, Indian man to all of us. "For all these parcels are *for you.*"

I have several times told you about our being dumb with amazement and terror and joy, and things like that, but I never remember us being dumber than we were when he said this.

The Indian Uncle went on: "I told an old friend of mine what a pleasant dinner I had with you, and about the three-penny-bit, and the divining-rod, and all that, and he sent all these odds and ends as presents for you. Some of the things came from India."

"Have you come from India, Uncle!" Noël asked; and when he said "Yes" we were all very much surprised, for we never thought of his being that sort of Indian. We thought he was the Red kind, and of course his not being accounted for his ignorance of beavers and things.

He got Eliza to help, and we took all the parcels into the nursery and he undid them and undid them and undid them, till the papers lay thick on the floor. Father came too and sat in the Guy Fawkes' chair. I cannot begin to tell you all the things that kind friend of Uncle's had sent us. He must be a very agreeable person.

There were toys for the kids and model engines for Dick and me, and a lot of books, and Japanese china tea-sets for the girls, red and white and gold—there were sweets by the pound and by the box—and long yards and yards of soft silk from India, to make frocks for the girls—and a real Indian sword for Oswald and a book of Japanese pictures for Noël, and some ivory chessmen for Dicky: the castles of the chessmen are elephant-and-castles. There is a railway station called that; I never knew what it meant before. The

brown paper and string parcels had boxes of games in them
—and big cases of preserved fruits and things. And the
shabby old newspaper parcels and the boxes had the Indian
things in. I never saw so many beautiful things before. There
were carved fans and silver bangles and strings of amber
beads, and necklaces of uncut gems—turquoises and garnets,
the Uncle said they were—and shawls and scarves of silk,
and cabinets of brown and gold, and ivory boxes and silver
trays, and brass things. The Uncle kept saying, "This is for
you, young man," or "Little Alice will like this fan," or
"Miss Dora would look well in this green silk, I think. Eh!
—what?"

And Father looked on as if it was a dream, till the Uncle
suddenly gave him an ivory paper-knife and a box of cigars,
and said, "My old friend sent you these, Dick; he's an old
friend of yours too, he says." And he winked at my Father,
for H. O. and I saw him. And my Father winked back,
though he has always told us not to.

That was a wonderful day. It was a treasure, and no mistake! I never saw such heaps and heaps of presents, like
things out of a fairy-tale—and even Eliza had a shawl. Perhaps she deserved it, for she did cook the rabbit and the pudding; and Oswald says it is not her fault if her nose turns
up and she does not brush her hair. I do not think Eliza likes
brushing things. It is the same with the carpets. But Oswald
tries to make allowances even for people who do not wash
their ears.

The Indian Uncle came to see us often after that, and
his friend always sent us something. Once he tipped us a
sovereign each—the Uncle brought it; and once he sent us
money to go to the Crystal Palace, and the Uncle took us;
and another time to a circus; and when Christmas was near
the Uncle said—

"You remember when I dined with you, some time ago,

you promised to dine with me some day, if I could ever afford to give a dinner-party. Well I'm going to have one—a Christmas party. Not on Christmas Day, because every one goes home then—but on the day after. Cold mutton and rice pudding. You'll come? Eh!—what?"

We said we should be delighted, if Father had no objection, because that is the proper thing to say, and the poor Indian, I mean the Uncle, said, "No, your Father won't object—he's coming too, bless your soul!"

We all got Christmas presents for the Uncle. The girls made him a handkerchief case and a comb bag, out of some of the pieces of silk he had given them. I got him a knife with three blades; H. O. got a siren whistle, a very strong one, and Dicky joined with me in the knife and Noël would give the Indian ivory box that Uncle's friend had sent on the wonderful Fairy Cab day. He said it was the very nicest thing he had, and he was sure Uncle wouldn't mind his not having bought it with his own money.

I think Father's business must have got better—perhaps Uncle's friend put money in it and that did it good, like feeding the starving. Anyway we all had new suits, and the girls had the green silk from India made into frocks, and on Boxing Day we went in two cabs—Father and the girls in one, and us boys in the other.

We wondered very much where the Indian Uncle lived, because we had not been told. And we thought when the cab began to go up the hill towards the Heath that perhaps the Uncle lived in one of the poky little houses up at the top of Greenwich. But the cab went right over the Heath and in at some big gates, and through a shrubbery all white with frost like a fairy forest, because it was Christmas time. And at last we stopped before one of those jolly, big, ugly red houses with a lot of windows, that are so comfortable inside, and on the steps was the Indian Uncle, looking very big and grand, in a blue cloth coat and yellow sealskin waistcoat, with a bunch of seals hanging from it.

"I wonder whether he has taken a place as butler here?" said Dicky. "A poor, broken-down man——"

Noël thought it was very likely, because he knew that in these big houses there were always thousands of stately butlers.

The Uncle came down the steps and opened the cab door himself, which I don't think butlers would expect to have to do. And he took us in. It was a lovely hall, with bear and tiger skins on the floor, and a big clock with the faces of the sun and moon dodging out when it was day or night, and Father Time with a scythe coming out at the hours, and the name on it was "Flint. Ashford. 1776"; and there was a fox eating a stuffed duck in a glass case, and horns of stags and other animals over the doors.

"We'll just come into my study first," said the Uncle, "and wish each other a Merry Christmas." So then we knew he wasn't the butler, but it must be his own house, for only the master of the house has a study.

His study was not much like Father's. It had hardly any books, but swords and guns and newspapers and a great many boots, and boxes half unpacked, with more Indian things bulging out of them.

We gave him our presents and he was awfully pleased. Then he gave us his Christmas presents. You must be tired of hearing about presents, but I must remark that all the Uncle's presents were watches; there was a watch for each of us, with our names engraved inside, all silver except H. O.'s, and that was a Waterbury, "To match his boots," the Uncle said. I don't know what he meant.

Then the Uncle looked at Father, and Father said, "You tell them, sir."

So the Uncle coughed and stood up and made a speech. He said—

"Ladies and gentlemen, we are met together to discuss an important subject which has for some weeks engrossed the attention of the honourable member opposite and myself."

I said, "Hear, hear," and Alice whispered, "What happened to the guinea-pig?" Of course you know the answer to that.

The Uncle went on—

"I am going to live in this house, and as it's rather big for me, your Father has agreed that he and you shall come and live with me. And so, if you're agreeable, we're all going to live here together, and, please God it'll be a happy home for us all. Eh!—what?"

He blew his nose and kissed us all round. As it was Christmas I did not mind, though I am much too old for it on other dates. Then he said, "Thank you all very much for your presents; but I've got a present here I value more than anything else I have."

I thought it was not quite polite of him to say so, till I saw that what he valued so much was a threepenny-bit on his watch-chain, and, of course, I saw it must be the one we had given him.

He said, "You children gave me that when you thought I was the poor Indian, and I'll keep it as long as I live. And I've asked some friends to help us to be jolly, for this is our house-warming, Eh!—what?"

Then he shook Father by the hand, and they blew their noses; and then Father said, "Your Uncle has been most kind —most——"

But Uncle interrupted by saying, "Now, Dick, no nonsense!"

Then H. O. said, "Then you're not poor at all?" as if he were very disappointed.

The Uncle replied, "I have enough for my simple wants,

thank you, H. O.; and your Father's business will provide him with enough for yours. Eh!—what?"

Then we all went down and looked at the fox thoroughly, and made the Uncle take the glass off so that we could see it all round; and then the Uncle took us all over the house, which is the most comfortable one I have ever been in. There is a beautiful portrait of Mother in Father's sitting-room. The Uncle must be very rich indeed. This ending is like what happens in Dickens's books; but I think it was much jollier to happen like a book, and it shows what a nice man the Uncle is, the way he did it all.

Think how flat it would have been if the Uncle had said, when we first offered him the one and threepence farthing, "Oh, I don't want your dirty one and threepence! I'm very rich indeed." Instead of which he saved up the news of his wealth till Christmas, and then told us all in one glorious burst. Besides, I can't help it if it is like Dickens, because it happens this way. Real life is often something like books.

Presently, when we had seen the house, we were taken into the drawing-room, and there was Mrs. Leslie, who gave us the shillings and wished us good hunting, and Lord Tottenham, and Albert-next-door's Uncle—and Albert-next-door, and his Mother (I'm not very fond of her), and best of all our own Robber and his two kids, and our Robber had a new suit on. The Uncle told us he had asked the people who had been kind to us, and Noël said, "Where is my noble editor that I wrote the poetry to?"

The Uncle said he had not had the courage to ask a strange editor to dinner; but Lord Tottenham was an old friend of Uncle's, and he had introduced Uncle to Mrs. Leslie, and that was how he had the pride and pleasure of welcoming her to our house-warming. And he made her a bow like you see on a Christmas card.

Then Alice asked, "What about Mr. Rosenbaum? He was kind; it would have been a pleasant surprise for him."

But everybody laughed, and Uncle said—

"Your father has paid him the sovereign he lent you. I don't think he could have borne another pleasant surprise."

And I said there was the butcher, and he was really kind; but they only laughed, and Father said you could not ask all your business friends to a private dinner.

Then it was dinner-time, and we thought of Uncle's talk about cold mutton and rice. But it was a beautiful dinner, and I never saw such a dessert! We had ours on plates to take away into another sitting-room, which was much jollier than sitting round the table with the grown-ups. But the Robber's kids stayed with their Father. They were very shy and frightened, and said hardly anything, but looked all about with very bright eyes. H. O. thought they were like white mice; but afterwards we got to know them very well, and in the end they were not so mousy. And there is a good deal of interesting stuff to tell about them; but I shall put all that in another book, for there is no room for it in this one. We played desert islands all the afternoon and drank Uncle's health in ginger wine. It was H. O. that upset his over Alice's green silk dress, and she never even rowed him. Brothers ought not to have favourites, and Oswald would never be so mean as to have a favourite sister, or, if he had, wild horses should not make him tell who it was.

And now we are to go on living in the big house on the Heath, and it is very jolly.

Mrs. Leslie often comes to see us, and our own Robber and Albert-next-door's uncle. The Indian Uncle likes him because he has been in India too and is brown; but our Uncle does not like Albert-next-door. He says he is a muff. And I am to go to Rugby, and so are Noël and H. O., and perhaps to Balliol afterwards. Balliol is my Father's college. It has two separate coats of arms, which many other colleges are not allowed. Noël is going to be a poet and Dicky wants to go into Father's business.

The Uncle is a real good old sort; and just think, we should never have found him if we hadn't made up our minds to be Treasure Seekers!

Noël made a poem about it—

> Lo! the poor Indian from lands afar,
> Comes where the treasure seekers are;
> We looked for treasure, but we find
> The best treasure of all is the Uncle good and kind.

I thought it was rather rot, but Alice would show it to the Uncle, and he liked it very much. He kissed Alice and he smacked Noël on the back, and he said, "I don't think *I've* done so badly either, if you come to that, though I was never a regular professional treasure seeker. Eh!—what?"

THE END